SATAN
SATANISM
AND
WITCHCRAFT

Dear Fellow Member:

Please accept this volume, a special Members' Edition of *Satan, Satanism and Witchcraft,* as a token of my appreciation for your interest in this ministry.

Because of your faithfulness in supporting the RADIO BIBLE CLASS we have been able to continue "telling the story of Jesus" by means of radio, television, and the printed page.

It is my prayer that this book will give you a greater awareness of the forces of evil in the world today. May these studies also encourage you to "Put on the whole armor of God, that ye may be able to stand against the wiles of the devil" (Eph. 6:11).

Thank you for your fellowship with us in the work of the Gospel.

RICHARD W. DEHAAN
Teacher, RADIO BIBLE CLASS

SATAN SATANISM AND WITCHCRAFT

by

RICHARD W. DEHAAN

with

HERBERT VANDER LUGT

ZONDERVAN PUBLISHING HOUSE
A DIVISION OF THE ZONDERVAN CORPORATION
GRAND RAPIDS, MICHIGAN

Contents

Preface

Anton Szandor La Vey is the "pastor" of the First Satanic Church in San Francisco, and devil worship is being practiced actively throughout the western world. Does a real, personal devil actually exist? If so, where did he come from, what is he like, and how does he operate?

The late Bishop James A. Pike, grieving over the suicide death of his son Jim, observed strange occurrences in his Cambridge apartment which led him to think that his son was seeking to communicate with him. He attended a number of seances in which Jim allegedly spoke to him. Can the spirits of the dead send signals to the living? Are mediums able to establish contact with the souls of those who have gone to the "other side"? What really happens in a seance?

Mrs. Jeane Dixon is considered a prophetess by many people, and top leaders in government and industry consult her for information about the future. Does she really receive messages from God through tarot cards, the crystal ball, or astrological readings? What about astrology? Is it reliable? Is it a harmless pastime? Or is it a practice Christians must avoid?

Sybil Leek calls herself a witch, and believes she is able to contact and utilize powers from the invisible realm. She has gained an international reputation, and says that over eight million people in the world are witches. What about witchcraft? Is it merely a game some people play? Is it beneficial to humanity? Or is it evil and dangerous?

Universities are offering courses in occultism, and teams of scientists are investigating reports of mysterious magical phenomena all over the globe. They are baffled by some of the amazing incidents they encounter, and admit that present scientific knowledge cannot account for them. What should be the Christian's attitude toward magic?

In this book a sincere effort is made to give Biblical answers to questions like these. The first three chapters are a study of the explicit teaching of the Bible about Satan, evil spirits, and their battle strategy. The remaining portion consists of a report and analysis of current occultism in the light of the Scriptures.

It has been impossible for me to investigate the large amount of available information on this subject, so I assigned full responsibility of the last three chapters to Herbert Vander Lugt, Research Editor of the Radio Bible Class.

The Word of God may not provide a specific explanation for every problem one may encounter as he studies Satan, Satanism, and witchcraft, but it sheds much light on these subjects and offers practical guidelines by which God's children can avoid the dangers inherent in occultism.

This volume therefore is sent out with the prayer that it may instruct and help many people in these days of unrest, confusion, and fear.

RICHARD W. DE HAAN

1

The Origin, Fall, and Activity of Satan

An unexpected and amazing development of this enlightened age is the resurgence of interest in Satan and an increase in occultic activity. A few years ago most people assumed that the devil was dead in the same manner that some theologians recently have affirmed the death of God. It is now becoming increasingly apparent that these reports were premature. Satan is very much alive, and is actively involved in today's world. Though many scientists and philosophers still scoff at the idea of a personal devil, highly educated people all over the world meet regularly to worship Satan. Some groups, having dedicated themselves to the service of the devil, have committed brutal sacrificial slayings, while others engage in vile acts of immorality. Witchcraft, seances, and fortunetelling, for many years limited to areas of ignorance and superstition, are now discussed in highly respected magazines. Newspapers carry horoscopes, and multitudes consult them seriously every day. Prominent people have received a great deal of publicity by reporting the reception of personal messages from the spirits of the dead. The late Bishop Pike, for example, published a widely-read book telling of seances in which he purportedly talked with his dead son who had committed suicide. Others, claiming the ability to foretell the future, also have become the objects of widespread interest, and the name of Jeane Dixon comes to the minds of millions whenever the subject is mentioned. In Europe today, more people are making a livelihood through the practice of occultism than the total number engaged in the Christian ministry. Belief in the existence of an unseen spiritual realm to be entered at death, and which has an influence upon human life, has captivated the minds of multitudes. The millions involved with occultism are ignorant of the real nature of these mysterious and dangerous areas of investigation, and refuse to turn to the one source of truth regarding the kingdom of darkness.

The Bible, the holy Word of God, reveals the true nature of the supernatural. It teaches that two real spiritual worlds exist, one good and the other evil. It tells us that God is a Spirit (John 4:24), and that a great number of angels called "ministering spirits" (Heb. 1:14) worship Him in Heaven and carry out His assignments upon earth. The other invisible kingdom is evil, and is under the direction of Satan, who controls an organized host of wicked spirit beings. They are a formidable foe arrayed against God and His people, and the apostle Paul declared,

> For we wrestle not against flesh and blood, but against principalities, against powers, against the rulers of the darkness of this world, against spiritual wickedness in high places (Eph. 6:12).

All that can be known about the devil's origin, fall, and present activity is to be found in the Bible. Although it does not specifically answer every question we may ask, it tells us the important facts about him and his kingdom. He was once a glorious, sinless creature, but he rebelled against God, was cast out of Heaven to earth, and now leads his great army of spirit beings in a futile attempt to defeat God and destroy His people.

I. SATAN'S ORIGINAL STATE

The devil was created an angelic being of great beauty and splendor and at one time had great favor with God. Ezekiel describes him in his sinless state as follows,

> Son of man, take up a lamentation upon the king of Tyre, and say unto him, Thus saith the Lord God: Thou sealest up the sum, full of wisdom, and perfect in beauty.
>
> Thou hast been in Eden, the garden of God; every precious stone was thy covering, the sardius, topaz, and the diamond, the beryl, the onyx, and the jasper, the sapphire, the emerald, and the carbuncle, and gold; the workmanship of thy timbrels and of thy flutes was prepared in thee in the day that thou wast created.
>
> Thou art the anointed cherub that covereth, and I have set thee so; that wast upon the holy mountain of God; thou hast walked up and down in the midst of the stones of fire.
>
> Thou wast perfect in thy ways from the day that thou wast created, till iniquity was found in thee (Ezek. 28:12-15).

Although the prophet was addressing these words primarily to an earthly ruler, the king of Tyre, it is apparent that the full meaning of this prophecy is not exhausted by its reference to a flesh-and-blood monarch. The ultimate subject of Ezekiel's words was Satan, the real instigator of the king's pride and cruelty.

Many Bible students reject this interpretation of Ezekiel's dirge. They consider this viewpoint to be untenable and imaginative, and prefer to consider the prophet's description to be a highly figurative portrayal of the king of Tyre. Some even say this lamentation incorporates a well-known Tyrian myth about a primeval being who lived in the "Garden of God" until he was expulsed for pride and rebellion. It is unlikely, however, that the inspired prophet would incorporate a myth into his message of judgment. Then, too, many prophetic pronouncements contained a double perspective. Isaiah, for example, after giving a stern warning of impending disaster, told Ahaz that the Lord would give a sign that the message he had spoken was true.

> Therefore the Lord himself shall give you a sign; Behold, the virgin shall conceive, and bear a son, and shall call his name Immanuel.
> Butter and honey shall he eat, that he may know to refuse the evil, and choose the good.
> For before the child shall know to refuse the evil, and choose the good, the land that thou abhorrest shall be forsaken by both her kings (Isa. 7:14-16).

The fourteenth verse is a definite reference to Christ, the virgin-born Son of God, but verses fifteen and sixteen point to Maher-shalal-hash-baz, the infant son of Isaiah whose birth and early years are described in the following chapter. Before the lad was three years old, Pekah and Rezin, kings of Israel and Syria, had been executed as the prophet had predicted. Since this type of double reference is common in the prophetic Scriptures, it should not be thought strange that Ezekiel, in pronouncing judgment upon the king of Tyre, should also be alluding to Satan, who motivated the earthly monarch to his sinful pride and cruelty.

The prophet declared that in his original state Satan was a creature of great wisdom and beauty. He portrays the devil as having been in Eden, the garden of God, and describes him as having been lavishly adorned with jewels at that time. The translation in our King James Version also speaks of the "timbrels" and "flutes" prepared by him on the day he was created, and some Bible students have inferred from this that he had great musical ability and was given charge of the heavenly choirs which sang their praises to God. The Hebrew words, however, are difficult to translate, and most students are convinced that the words rendered "timbrels" and "flutes" more likely refer to the gold settings and engravings of his ornamental attire.

> . . . every precious stone was thy covering, the sardius, topaz, and the diamond, the beryl, the onyx, and the jasper, the sapphire, the emerald, and the carbuncle, and gold; the workmanship of thy timbrels and of thy flutes was prepared in thee in the day that thou wast created (Ezek. 28:13).

This exalted creature is also declared to be "the anointed cherub that covereth" (Ezek. 28:14), which indicates that God appointed him to have a place of special prominence in connection with his throne. The remainder of the verse, "thou wast upon the holy mountain of God; thou hast walked up and down in the midst of the stones of fire," indicates that before his sin, he was in the immediate presence of God's glorious holiness. In fact, he may have been the most exalted of all the angels, and the memory of this former glory could have been the reason Michael did not dare "bring against him a railing accusation" (Jude 9). Dr. Eric Sauer suggests the possibility that even before God created man He committed to Lucifer a position of authority in relation to the earth and its surrounding planets. For this reason Satan is called the "god of this world" in the New Testament.

II. SATAN'S REBELLION

This angelic creature of surpassing beauty and intelligence, however, initiated a rebellion against God. This explains the entrance of sin, suffering, and death into a universe which had been "good" as it came from God's creative hand. The Scriptures do not attempt to tell us why God permitted sin to invade His world, for His reasons are among the "secret things" which "belong unto the Lord our God" (Deut. 29:29). We cannot fully understand how or why an infinitely holy God brought about the possibility of evil, nor can we explain the origin of pride and rebellion against Him. But by faith we are assured that God is holy, wise, and loving. Our confidence in Him enables us to believe that behind His permission of sin, suffering, and death lies infinite holiness, wisdom, and goodness. The Bible simply affirms that the angel Lucifer, now called Satan, became proud and rebelled against his Maker. Here are the inspired words of Ezekiel.

> Thou wast perfect in thy ways from the day that thou wast created, till iniquity was found in thee.
> Thine heart was lifted up because of thy beauty; thou hast corrupted thy wisdom by reason of thy brightness; I will cast thee to the ground, I will lay thee before kings, that they may behold thee (Ezek. 28:15, 17).

Isaiah also speaks of this event in his dirge addressed to the king of Babylon, saying,

> How art thou fallen from heaven, O Lucifer, son of the morning! How art thou cut down to the ground, who didst weaken the nations!
> For thou hast said in thine heart, I will ascend into heaven, I will exalt my throne above the stars of God; I will sit also upon the mount of the congregation, in the sides of the north,
> I will ascend above the heights of the clouds, I will be like the Most High (Isa. 14:12-14).

The full import of this prophecy, like that of Ezekiel 28, cannot be limited to an earthly monarch. Lucifer, the daystar, succumbed to pride and revolted against God. Apparently many angels joined in the rebellion, for the Bible speaks of "angels that sinned" (2 Pet. 2:4), "angels who kept not their first estate" (Jude 6), and Revelation 12:4 in figurative language describes the red dragon (Satan) as pulling down a third of the stars (angels) from heaven with his tail.

Satan and his followers have been cast out of Heaven to the earth. They hate God and His people, and have neither desire for nor hope of salvation. The terms "evil" and "foul" are sometimes used to describe the evil spirits who make up Satan's army. Even the name "Satan" means adversary, and the word "devil" portrays him as one who accuses or criticizes. The Lord Jesus depicted the character of Satan when He said,

> He was a murderer from the beginning, and abode not in the truth, because there is no truth in him. When he speaketh a lie, he speaketh of his own; for he is a liar, and the father of it (John 8:44).

The fall of Lucifer, therefore, has made him an implacable enemy of God, a false accuser, and a liar whose every activity is marked by deceitfulness.

III. Satan's Present Activity and Certain Doom

The devil today is the leader of a vast host of evil spirits who are organized into a military-like structure. Paul wrote,

> For we wrestle not against flesh and blood, but against principalities, against powers, against the rulers of the darkness of this world, against spiritual wickedness in high places (Eph. 6:12).

Remember that Satan, though intelligent and powerful, is not omnipotent, omniscient, nor omnipresent. He can be in only one place at a time, but his myriads of assistants can largely make up for his inherent finiteness. With their help he tries to lead people into sinful practices and introduces false doctrine into the professing church.

Though fallen humanity possesses an evil nature, many of the completely inhuman and unnatural evils of society are at least in part traceable to the devil and his evil spirits. How else can we account for the insanity of drug addiction and homosexuality? Truly, the history of mankind testifies to the existence of the devil.

The widespread confusion and strife within the realm of professing Christendom is also partly due to Satanic activity. Surely the Bible cannot be blamed for the chaotic maze of beliefs and practices among those who call themselves Christians. While honest Biblical scholars may differ on certain matters of doctrine, the great central truths of the Christian faith as expressed in the early confessions are clearly taught in the Scriptures. The truth that God has eternally existed in three persons — Father, Son, and Holy Spirit — is plainly set forth. The great redemptive facts connected with Jesus Christ — His virgin birth, sinless life, atoning death, literal resurrection, and ascension into Heaven — are expressed so clearly that no one should misunderstand them. The way of salvation by grace through faith is so apparent that no one who reads the Bible should be confused. Why then all this hodgepodge of belief? Is it only because men are spiritually blind and unwilling to accept God's truth? No, the New Testament makes it clear that evil spirits play an influential part in promoting divisions and false teaching. The apostle Paul declared,

> Now the Spirit speaketh expressly that, in the latter times, some shall depart from the faith, giving heed to seducing spirits, and doctrines of demons (1 Tim. 4:1).

False teaching is definitely connected with evil spirits. Paul declares that they use hypocritical men with seared consciences,

> Speaking lies in hypocrisy, having their conscience seared with a hot iron,
> Forbidding to marry, and commanding to abstain from foods, which God hath created to be received with thanksgiving by them who believe and know the truth (1 Tim. 4:2, 3).

Evil spirits seek to divide and corrupt the church. They use professing Christians who deny basic Biblical truths such as the Trinity, the absolute deity and genuine humanity of Jesus Christ, His atoning death and literal resurrection, and salvation by grace through faith. For this reason, believers should always be on guard, and obey the exhortation of the apostle John who in his first epistle says, "Test the spirits whether they are of God; because many false prophets are gone out into the world" (1 John 4:1).

Most of the cults that have arisen in the last 200 years are propagating the same basic ideas that heretical groups taught in the days of the early church. These doctrines were repudiated then, but are continually being revived by the same evil spirits who first presented them to the minds of unscrupulous religionists.

The devil also seeks to keep men from believing on Jesus Christ. Though the Gospel includes some of the best-attested facts of all history, and though it has transformed the lives of millions who have believed its message, many still reject Jesus Christ. Such blindness is at least in part the work of Satan, for we are told that "the god of this age hath

blinded the minds of them who believe not, lest
the light of the glorious Gospel of Christ, who is
the image of God, should shine unto them" (2 Cor.
4:4). In addition, he tries to make people love the
earthly and temporal fashions of this world rather
than God, and through various forms of occultism
seeks to lead them away from Jesus Christ. These
aspects of Satan's activity will be discussed in detail
in the following chapters.

In spite of all of the devil's present power, however, we may be confident that he is a defeated foe
whose doom is sure. The writer of Hebrews tells
us that Jesus became identified with us in our humanity,

> . . . that through death he might destroy him
> that had the power of death, that is, the devil,
> And deliver them who, through fear of death,
> were all their lifetime subject to bondage (Heb.
> 2:14, 15).

The Lord Jesus sealed Satan's defeat and eternal
condemnation when He paid the full price for human sin on the cross and, as the God-man, destroyed the power of death by His resurrection.
Therefore, though the devil is still called "the god
of this world" and at this very time "goes about
like a roaring lion seeking whom he may devour,"
he knows he cannot win his war against God. In
fact, he cannot even cause a humble believer to
sin if that individual submits to God and opposes
the evil one. James declared,

> . . . God resisteth the proud, but giveth grace
> unto the humble.
> Submit yourselves, therefore, to God. Resist
> the devil, and he will flee from you (James 4:
> 6, 7).

The devil is far more powerful than any person,
and the individual who tries to defeat him in his

own strength will surely fail. The Christian who lives in daily submission to the Lord, however, can successfully resist every onslaught of Satan.

The prophetic Scriptures expressly depict Satan's final defeat. During the brief period of tribulation preceding our Lord's return to establish the Messianic Kingdom, a fearful display of demonic activity will be manifested (Rev. 9:1-21). The apostle Paul declares that Satan will work "all power and signs and lying wonders, and with all deceivableness of unrighteousness in them that perish . . ." (2 Thess. 2:9, 10). Revelation 16 states that evil spirits, working through Satan, Antichrist, and the false prophet, will deceive the leaders of the nations into thinking they can conquer the Lord Jesus Christ.

> And I saw three unclean spirits like frogs, come out of the mouth of the dragon, and out of the mouth of the beast, and out of the mouth of the false prophet.
> For they are the spirits of demons, working miracles, that go forth unto the kings of the earth and of the whole world, to gather them to the battle of that great day of God Almighty (Rev. 16:13, 14).

This desperate effort to defeat God will be completely unsuccessful. The Antichrist and the false prophet will be cast into the lake of fire, and their armies will be utterly destroyed (Rev. 19:11-21). The devil himself will be cast into the bottomless pit (Rev. 20:1-3) for 1000 years. He will then be released for a brief period, when he will once more gather his hosts for a final assault against God. This time Satan with all of his followers will be utterly defeated and cast into the Lake of Fire. Final victory belongs to God and His people, for His eternal purposes cannot be frustrated by the powers of darkness.

In summary, then, Satan was originally sinless and the most glorious of all created beings. But he led a rebellion against God, was cast out of Heaven to the earth, and now operates as the chief adversary of the Almighty. He leads an organized kingdom of evil spirits who joined him in the revolt, and exercises such great power and influence among men that the Bible calls him "the god of this age." The sentence of eternal damnation hangs over him, however, because Jesus paid the price for human sin on Calvary and destroyed the power of both death and Satan by His resurrection. The believer who lives in submission to the Holy Spirit can therefore successfully resist every attack of the evil one, and can possess the joyous assurance that final victory belongs to God and His people.

2

His Invisible Army

Twentieth-century man, in spite of all his scientific and technological advances, is baffled by unexplained forces existent in the universe. The naturalistic philosophy of the previous generation has been unable to account for all of the mysterious phenomena which have been observed. Many scientists believe that living beings may inhabit other galaxies, and highly educated men are seriously studying the reports of those who insist they have received communications from the dead. Men of science no longer scoff at the accounts of strange occurrences associated with witchcraft and occultic practices. Although they do not necessarily accept them as proof of the supernatural, many will admit they are manifestations of some kind of power they do not yet understand.

Christian theologians and scientists are not perplexed by such reports. They know that both God and Satan are very much alive. Though readily conceding that they cannot explain fully all the mysteries of life, they affirm with confidence the existence of God and an invisible host of intelligent supernatural beings. They are convinced that when one accepts the teachings of the Bible, he begins to understand many of the puzzling facts of existence. For example, the Bible tells of holy angels who dwell in Heaven (Matt. 18:10). It also mentions "angels that sinned" (2 Pet. 2:4), rebellious spirit beings who have been cast out of Heaven and now dwell in the atmosphere that surrounds the earth. We know this because Paul declared that Satan is "the prince of the power of the air" (Eph. 2:2), and the Greek word translated "air" was used to speak of the gaseous envelope that encircles our planet. These wicked beings apparently have unlimited access to earth, and actively influence every area of human endeavor. Because they do not possess physical bodies, we cannot detect them through our senses of sight, hearing, touch, taste, or smell. We do have evidence of their presence, however, for the Word of God gives us information regarding their identification, their nature, and their function.

I. THE BIBLICAL IDENTIFICATION

Various terms are used in the Bible to denote the evil spirit beings who followed Satan in his initial act of rebellion against God. It refers to "angels that sinned" (2 Pet. 2:4) and "angels who kept not their first estate" (Jude 6), and many times mentions "spirits" and "demons." Some scholars believe that these demons must be distinguished from the "angels that sinned" and the "angels who kept not their first estate." They contend that the heavenly beings who joined Satan in his revolt against God are fallen angels, but that demons are disembodied spirits of physical and moral creatures who once lived upon the earth. But these Bible students disagree regarding an exact identification of the demons. Some say they are the spirits of pre-Adamic beings similar to man, while others identify them as the spirits of the "giants" who were destroyed in the great flood of Noah's day.

If one thinks that demons are the spirits of man-like beings who lived before Adam, then he will no doubt interpret Genesis 1:2 as a declaration that the original earth, inhabited by the creatures, was cataclysmically destroyed. Genesis 1:2 is then translated as follows: "And the earth *became* without form and void. . . ." This theory, while attractive in that it permits a literal interpretation of the days in Genesis 1, must be acknowledged as only a hypothesis. Most Hebrew scholars reject this interpretation because Genesis 1:2 begins with a grammatical construction which makes it highly unlikely that Genesis 1:1 and 1:2 are separated by millions of years. Then, too, the verb translated "became" almost always has the meaning "was." But even if we accept this theory, and believe that a race of man-like beings inhabited the prehistoric earth, we would have no basis for thinking that their spirits are now free to roam about as the enemies of mankind.

Other Bible scholars maintain that demons are the spirits of the "giants" who lived upon the earth in the days of Noah. They refer to Genesis 6, contending that these "giants" were produced when fallen angels, called the "sons of God," married the "daughters of men."

> And it came to pass, when men began to multiply on the face of the earth, and daughters were born unto them,
>   That the sons of God saw the daughters of men that they were fair; and they took them wives of all whom they chose.
>   There were giants in the earth in those days; and also after that, when the sons of God came in unto the daughters of men, and they bore children to them, the same became mighty men who were of old, men of renown (Gen. 6:1, 2, 4).

It is necessary for proponents of this theory to believe that fallen angels became male human beings who married women, produced a mongrel offspring, and took over the role of father in the family. They theorize that Satan hoped thereby to frustrate God's redemptive plan. The Lord had promised salvation through Christ to human beings only — not for angels or a mixed half-human and half-angelic race. Christ could not have been born to offspring of these corrupted creatures or provide redemption for them. Thus God's plan of redemption would have been thwarted. In addition, both Jude and Peter in their epistles refer to a sin committed by angels, and their words can be blended very nicely into this concept. Jude writes,

> And the angels who kept not their first estate, but left their own habitation, he hath reserved in everlasting chains under darkness unto the judgment of the great day.
> Even as Sodom and Gomorrah, and the cities about them in like manner, giving themselves over to fornication, and going after strange flesh, are set forth for an example, suffering the vengeance of eternal fire (Jude 6, 7).

The words "in like manner" (verse 7) are taken to mean that the sin of the angels in having sexual relationships with women was an unnatural act, comparable to sodomy.

Peter tells of angels assigned to *Tartaros,* the nether world the Greeks considered to be lower than Hades.

> For if God spared not the angels that sinned, but cast them down to hell [Gk. Tartaros], and delivered them into chains of darkness, to be reserved unto judgment (2 Pet. 2:4).

Again, it does not take a great deal of imagination to see how these words of Peter may be applied to the wicked angels who committed the monstrous sin of attempting to make mongrels of the human race.

Many Bible students, however, reject this interpretation of Genesis 6. Since angels are non-material beings, it would be necessary for them to create physical bodies for themselves capable of impregnating a female member of the human race. This would require nothing less than a creative miracle, and the Bible indicates that this power belongs only to God. In addition, it is not necessary to interpret the statements in Jude and 2 Peter as a reference to sexual sin on the part of the fallen angels. Jude's use of the expression "going after strange flesh" may be figurative language representing spiritual fornication. The prophets often depicted Israel's unfaithfulness to Jehovah in this manner. Peter's statement that the angels who sinned have been assigned to *Tartaros* may be a simple declaration that all sinning angels have been designated to this place, and that they are even now under chains of *moral* and *spiritual* darkness.

The Bible gives little information regarding the origin of demons. We can state with absolute certainty only that they are fallen spirit beings who have committed themselves to Satan and that they hate God and seek to harm His people. No clear distinction can be made between fallen angels and demons, for they are all evil spirits. Some of our questions must remain unanswered, but the Lord has given ample revelation to warn us that these invisible enemies are far too great and powerful for us to defeat in our own strength, and that we can successfully wage war against them only as we live in continual dependence upon the Lord.

II. The Characteristics of Demons

Unlike apocryphal and rabbinical literature, the Biblical description of evil spirits avoids the unusual and grotesque. The Bible does, however, present us with a clear picture of their activity and tells us how to resist them effectively.

In the first place, it declares that demons or fallen angels are non-material beings. They do not possess bodies like humans, and therefore are repeatedly called "spirits." Matthew, for example, says,

> When the evening was come, they brought unto him many that were possessed with demons; and he cast out the spirits with his word, and healed all that were sick (Matt. 8:16).

Jesus stated that the Creator is not made up of physical substance when He said, "God is a Spirit" (John 4:24). Later, when His frightened disciples thought He was a ghost, He told them their fears were groundless, for "a *spirit* hath not flesh and bones, as ye see me have" (Luke 24:39). Paul had in mind the non-physical nature of Satan and his army of evil spirits when he said that our warfare is "not against flesh and blood, but against principalities, against powers, against the rulers of the darkness of this world, against spiritual wickedness in high places" (Eph. 6:12). Satan's demonic hordes are spirit beings, and therefore more dangerous than the "flesh and blood" enemies we may encounter in our daily lives.

Second, the Bible portrays demons as highly intelligent creatures. They recognized Christ when He was here upon earth, and knew they could not have fellowship with Him. Luke tells us about an evil spirit who is an example of this.

> When he saw Jesus, he cried out, and fell down before him, and with a loud voice said, What have I to do with thee, Jesus, thou Son of God, most high? I beseech thee, torment me not (Luke 8:28).

The fallen spirits are also aware of their ultimate defeat, for James declared, "The demons also believe, and tremble" (James 2:19). They are, of course, finite creatures, and even Satan is limited in knowledge. He has myriads of evil spirit followers, however, and they are able to give him information on almost any person and circumstance in which he is interested. In this manner he can find out much of what he wants to know. Truly, believers in Christ can never successfully cope with Satan and his hosts without special help from the Lord. Therefore, we must humbly look to God for wisdom and strength to resist the attacks of our invisible enemies.

Third, the world of evil spirits is cruel. These creatures hate God and all who have placed their trust in Him. They seem to find delight in causing human grief and pain. For example, Matthew tells us that a man who was both blind and dumb suffered these afflictions because a demon had entered his body.

> Then was brought unto him one possessed with a demon, blind, and dumb; and he healed him, insomuch that the blind and dumb both spoke and saw (Matt. 12:22).

Matthew, Mark, and Luke all tell the story of two demented men who lived in the country of the Gerasenes, and indicate that their insanity was the result of demonic invasion of their personalities. Luke, the beloved physician, writes of a woman who was bent over with some crippling disease, saying that she had "a spirit of infirmity." He adds that Jesus said she had been bound by Satan.

> And he was teaching in one of the synagogues on the sabbath.
> And, behold, there was a woman who had a

spirit of infirmity eighteen years, and was bowed together, and could in no way lift herself up.

And when Jesus saw her, he called her to him, and said unto her, Woman, thou art loosed from thine infirmity.

And he laid his hands on her; and immediately she was made straight, and glorified God.

And the ruler of the synagogue answered with indignation, because Jesus had healed on the sabbath day, and said unto the people, There are six days in which men ought to work; in them, therefore, come and be healed, and not on the sabbath day.

The Lord then answered him, and said, Thou hypocrite, doth not each one of you on the sabbath loose his ox or his ass from the stall, and lead him away to watering?

And ought not this woman, being a daughter of Abraham, whom Satan hath bound, lo, these eighteen years, be loosed from this bond on the sabbath day?

And when he had said these things, all his adversaries were ashamed; and all the people rejoiced for all the glorious things that were done by him (Luke 13:10-17).

While the gospel writers make it clear that not all illness is the work of Satan and demons, they do point out that much human suffering is the result of demonic activity.

Finally, the Bible tells us that all fallen angels or evil spirits are confirmed in their wickedness. Though they "believe and tremble," they will never repent, never seek forgiveness, and never pray for holiness or purity. Though they know that Jesus is the Christ, they never really worship Him. They must acknowledge that He is stronger than they, and may occasionally render Him token submission, but inwardly they hate Him and keenly resent His authority over them. In fact, their nature is so totally evil that the term "unclean" often is applied to them. (See Matt. 10:1; Mark 1:27; 3:11; Luke 4:36; Acts 8:7; Rev. 16:13.) They apparently delight in sin, find great pleasure in leading men and women to commit evil deeds, and possess no feelings of guilt nor desire for deliverance.

III. Demon Possession

The New Testament includes a number of references to people afflicted with what we term "demon possession." Skeptics have looked upon these accounts as reflections of the ignorance and superstition prevalent during the time of our Lord's ministry. Others contend that Jesus, knowing that the public attributed disease and insanity to evil spirits, was only accommodating Himself to their way of thinking. A careful reading of the gospels and the book of Acts, however, indicates that Christ and His apostles accepted the reality of evil spirits, and taught their followers to fear them. It is therefore imperative that we turn to the Scriptures to find out exactly what demon possession is, the measure of human responsibility involved, and the believer's course of action when he encounters a demon-possessed individual.

A. *The nature of demon possession.* A demon-possessed person is one who has been invaded by evil spirits. They may control his body, his mind, or both. Sometimes they produce only physical illness, but at other times their wretched victims are grossly immoral, speak blasphemously, and exhibit supernatural strength. They obviously have been mastered, mind and body, by a superior force.

In understanding the nature of demon possession, we must first take note that the Bible cites a number of demon-produced illnesses with all the characteristics of known diseases. The gospel writers were careful to distinguish between natural and demon-caused afflictions, as is evident in the first chapter of Mark.

> And in the evening, when the sun did set, they brought unto him all that were diseased, and those who were possessed with demons.
> And he healed many that were sick of diverse diseases, and cast out many demons; and permitted not the demons to speak, because they knew him (Mark 1:32, 34).

When sickness did not involve evil spirits, the Lord restored health to the individual with no mention of demons. If the illness was the result of demonic invasion, however, Jesus healed by commanding the evil spirits to leave the victim's body. For example, the boy who had a deaf and dumb spirit (Mark 9:14-29) manifested the symptoms that mark epilepsy, but in healing him, the Lord rebuked a "foul spirit." When it left, the spirit threw the lad into violent convulsions. Matthew gives the account of a man afflicted with dumbness whom Jesus healed by casting out an indwelling demon (Matt. 9:32-35). Christ also cured a man who was blind and dumb by ordering the demon to leave his body (Matt. 12:22). Luke, telling of a woman who had been seriously crippled for eighteen years, said she had "a spirit of infirmity" (Luke 13:11). After healing her, the Lord Jesus spoke of her as "a daughter of Abraham, whom Satan hath bound, lo, these eighteen years" (Luke 13:16). In none of these instances did the demons lead the individual into blasphemous speech or immoral conduct. The afflictions were only physical in nature.

In addition to causing many varieties of physical suffering, evil spirits often took control of a person's mental faculties and organs of speech. The two wild men in Gadara, appearing to be insane, possessed strength far beyond that of ordinary men, lived in tombs with the gruesome remains of dead bodies, and were so feared that people avoided the territory they inhabited (Matt. 8:28-34; Luke 8:26-36). When they saw Jesus, they cried out, "What have we to do with thee, Jesus, thou Son of God? Art thou come here to torment us before the time?" (Matt. 8:29). These words, though coming from the mouths of the men, were obviously spoken by the evil spirits. Luke, focusing his attention upon the more prominent of the two, tells us that after the Lord had cast the demons out of the man, he was found by the people of the area "sitting at the feet of Jesus, clothed, and in his right mind" (Luke 8:35). This kind of demon possession, in which the victim could not control his own mind and speech, was more spectacular, but also more tragic, than that which manifested itself in physical illness alone. The person who experienced only bodily affliction could still make intelligent choices, but the others had no control over what they said and did.

B. *Human responsibility and demon possession.* Bible students are not agreed concerning the extent of human responsibility in demon possession. It appears that sometimes the individual was in no way accountable for this invasion of his personality. The boy who suffered seizures similar to those of epilepsy had been afflicted from early childhood (Mark 9:21). These convulsions sometimes came upon the lad as he was standing by water or fire, and almost cost him his life when he fell. Since this physical affliction came upon him at such a young age, it would seem that he did nothing to cause demonic invasion of his body.

On the other hand, many believe that God would

not permit evil spirits to take over a human personality unless that individual first weakened his will by voluntarily yielding to temptation. If one accepts this premise, he will consider those who are violent, unclean, and blasphemous because of demon possession to be partly responsible for their present state. They likely made themselves susceptible to demonic invasion of their personalities by persisting in sinful practices.

C. *The believer's authority over demons.* The Lord Jesus cast out demons on numerous occasions. Eight of the recorded miracles involve demon expulsion, but the gospels indicate that He exercised this power many other times. Luke declares,

> And demons also came out of many, crying out, and saying, Thou art Christ, the Son of God. And he, rebuking them, did not allow them to speak; for they knew that he was Christ (Luke 4:41).

The gospel writers seem to indicate that whenever Christ encountered a demon-possessed individual, He expelled the evil spirit without difficulty. As the Lord of the invisible world, Jesus spoke with absolute authority, and the demon had no alternative but to do what He commanded. Mark records,

> And he healed many that were sick of diverse diseases, and cast out many demons; and permitted not the demons to speak, because they knew him (Mark 1:34).

The Lord also commissioned the Twelve to exercise authority over evil spirits. In chapter 3 of Mark's gospel we read:

> And he appointed twelve, that they should be with him, and that he might send them forth to preach,
> And to have authority to heal sicknesses, and to cast out demons (Mark 3:14, 15).

On another occasion, He gave this power to a larger group, for He sent out seventy disciples on a special mission, and they returned in joyous excitement, saying, "Lord, even the demons are subject unto us through thy name" (Luke 10:17).

Today the power to resist and overcome evil spirits in the name of Jesus belongs to every believer. The Holy Spirit indwells even the weakest Christian (1 Cor. 6:19), and the least gifted among those who trust in Christ have received all the benefits of salvation. James makes it clear that a believer who humbly trusts God can cause Satan, the supreme ruler of the demon world, to flee.

> But he giveth more grace. Wherefore he saith, God resisteth the proud, but giveth grace unto the humble.
> Submit yourselves, therefore, to God. Resist the devil, and he will flee from you (James 4: 6, 7).

If one who knows Christ can successfully resist the comander-in-chief of the demonic hordes, he certainly can overcome the soldiers who make up the army of Satan when they seek to lead him into sin.

Casting demons out of an afflicted person is another matter, however, and believers must exercise extreme care when they are confronted with demon possession. These evil spirits may be very powerful, and sometimes can be expelled only after a time of heart searching and earnest prayer on the part of the Christians who are seeking to deliver the possessed person. Mark tells us of an occasion when a father was disappointed in the apostles, who themselves had become discouraged when they were unable to help a demon-possessed boy. Jesus rebuked them for their spiritual lack, saying, "This kind can come forth by nothing, but by prayer" (Mark 9:29). (The words "and fasting," which occur in our King James Version, are not found in the best Greek manuscripts. Furthermore, there would have been no opportunity for the disciples to fast in connection with their attempt to heal this boy.) This Scripture passage certainly indicates that no believer should attempt to cast out demons unless he exercises strong faith, renounces sin, and lives in continuous fellowship with the Lord. Missionaries who have encountered demon possession say that sometimes the victory is won by a simple command uttered in the name of the Lord Jesus. (The phrase "in the name of the Lord Jesus" really means, "by the authority of Jesus.") In other instances, however, God's servants have found it necessary to engage in a period of prayer and confession of sin. Nevius, in his book entitled *Demon Possession and Allied Themes,* recounts numerous instances of demon possession which he and his co-workers in China found during the last half of the nineteenth century. This man's character and theological position make him a trustworthy source of information. He said that demons often spoke to the missionaries as they were about to cast them out of a hapless victim, sometimes pleaded for mercy, often resisted, but always were forced to leave after Christians prayed together and gave the command in the name of the Lord Jesus. Representatives of Christ in many other lands dominated by heathen religions discover a great deal of demon possession. They also are unanimous in declaring that through prayer and a command "in the name of the Lord Jesus" they have been able to expel the evil spirits.

Christians must exercise caution whenever they encounter someone who seems to be demon-possessed. In the first place, one ought to be sure the person is suffering from demon possession rather than a condition resulting from some physical, psychological, or spiritual disorder. Some people are greatly harmed when they are wrongly told that they are demon-possessed. They actually need help from a medical doctor, psychiatrist, or spiritual counselor, but instead keep on seeking to expel evil spirits.

A "possessed" person may have symptoms much like those that are apparent in the mentally ill. He may be deeply melancholic or depressed, appear to be withdrawn from reality, or may manifest emotions that range from ecstatic joy to violent screaming or wild ferocity. These various states may present themselves from time to time during "attacks." Demon possession may be distinguished from insanity, however, by observing the manner in which the afflicted person speaks. An insane individual may have a mistaken concept of his own identity, wear clothing by which he attempts to look like the person he thinks himself to be, but speak in his own voice, and in such a manner that one can tell he is doing only a superficial impersonation of the individual he thinks himself to be. A demon-possessed person, on the other hand, is obviously controlled by the indwelling evil spirit. The wicked being may use a language or dialect the individual never knew, and sometimes will name himself. Therefore, one should carefully note the symptoms of a disturbed person, never making the diagnosis of demon possession on the basis of a superficial judgment.

If a believer should meet a demon-possessed individual, he would be unwise to make a frontal attack upon the powers of darkness by immediately issuing a command in the name of the Lord Jesus. Dr. Kurt Koch, an evangelical Christian who has made a lifetime study of Satan and occultic activities, declares that whenever Christians lightly engage in an effort to cast out demons, they run the risk of being attacked by evil spirits. Such people often suffer deep spiritual depression and find themselves in an attitude of complete hopelessness. Since this is true, a believer should band together with others in a time of prayer, and no effort should be made to expel the evil spirits until the Holy Spirit prompts someone to issue the command.

Unbelievers and adherents of the non-Christian religions apparently can command evil spirits without suffering bad consequences. Archeologists have found manuscripts containing incantaticns and magical formulas for the expulsion of demons; and today in the Philippines and other countries of the far East, as well as in some areas of South America and Africa, pagan religious leaders seriously perform rituals to ward off or cast out evil spirits. Sometimes they beat the person who is demon-possessed, prick him with needles, or even burn portions of his body, thinking that this pain will drive out the evil spirits.

The Jews in Christ's day also used spells, magical phrases, and religious rituals to expel demons. That they sometimes appeared to be successful is clear, for Jesus said,

> . . . if I, by Beelzebub, cast out demons, by whom do your sons cast them out? Therefore, they shall be your judges (Matt. 12:27).

In this statement the Lord Jesus acknowledged that evil spirits sometimes left the bodies of their victims when incantations, spells, or magical rites were used by Jewish religious leaders. But Christ did not say these men accomplished their goal by the power of God, nor did He imply that they were actually doing damage to the cause of Satan. He was answering the charge that He was casting out demons in the power of Beelzebub, the prince of the demons. He declared that if such were the case, the kingdom of Satan would be divided against itself. Actually, the exorcists, whether Jewish or pagan, did not really possess authority over the invisible world, but the evil spirits merely cooperated with them, leaving the bodies of some of their victims to give the appearance that they had been forced out. By working with these unbelieving sorcerers the devil aided his own cause. The demons either temporarily left the person, only to return a short time later, or entered the body of some other victim.

No one should attempt to deal with the forces of evil by using the name of Jesus unless he is a child of God. Luke, in Acts 19, graphically portrays the seriousness of hypocritically dealing with the powers of darkness. Seven sons of Sceva, a professional exorcist who had no personal faith in Christ, tried to combine the words "in the name of Jesus" with their magical formula. The evil spirits, recognizing that these impostors had no right to use Jesus' name, reacted in a violent manner. The demon-possessed individual attacked these men with superhuman strength, so that with torn clothing and bleeding bodies they fled from the house.

D. *The frequency of demon possession.* The record of history establishes without a doubt that demon possession was known before the Lord Jesus came to earth, and the testimony of missionaries indicates that it has continued down through the centuries. The public ministry of Christ, however, was accompanied by an outburst of demon possession unparalleled in history. It seems that

Satan threw all his power into his battle with Jesus Christ. True, the devil is not omniscient, but he knew that Christ had come to earth to atone for sin, conquer death, and bring about the defeat of evil. John tells us that "the Son of God was manifested, that he might destroy the works of the devil" (1 John 3:8). Satan used every device at his disposal to frustrate the purpose of God in Christ. Subtle temptations, the wrath and wickedness of men, and a rash of demonic activity were part of his vain effort to prevent Jesus from performing the work He had come to accomplish.

Demon possession gradually subsided during the first century A.D., and usually is not conspicuous in areas where a fairly large percentage of people have placed their faith in Jesus Christ. It appears that demons are hesitant to enter the bodies of people when informed believers are likely to cast them out in the name of Christ. Luke's account of the wild man at Gadara may give us a clue as to their reason for this hesitancy. The demons who had inhabited this man knew if Jesus expulsed them, they would enter the "deep." The Greek word used by Luke is the same one that is translated "bottomless pit" seven times in the book of the Revelation. We read,

> And Jesus asked him, saying, What is thy name? And he said, Legion; because many demons were entered into him.
>
> And they besought him that he would not command them to go out into the *deep*.
>
> And there was there an herd of many swine, feeding on the mountain; and they besought him that he would allow them to enter into them. And he permitted them (Luke 8:30-32).

Revelation 9 tells us that at some future time the "bottomless pit" will be opened, and a great army of evil spirits will be set free to plague mankind. It is at least a possibility that whenever demons are cast out of a human being in the name of Jesus, they are sent to the bottomless pit, and will not be released until shortly before Christ returns to establish His kingdom. The realization that they will lose their freedom as members of the army of the "prince of the power of the air," and be confined in the pit for an indefinite period of time, makes them hesitant to take possession of human beings. The risk is too great in an area where Christians exercise their authority in the name of Christ.

People who live in civilized countries where the Gospel has been known for centuries should not rule out the possibility of demon possession, however, just because it has not been a common occurrence in these areas. Satan and his cohorts may conclude that most people, even professing Christians, will not recognize this phenomenon when they meet it. Therefore, as this age draws to a close, Satan may once again become very active in entering human bodies and controlling personalities. He will hope that the majority of mankind will either be deceived into following him or find a naturalistic explanation for the activities of the demons. This supernatural manifestation of the power of Satan and evil spirits is clearly predicted by the apostle Paul. In his second letter to the Thessalonian believers he declares that just before Christ returns in glory, the devil will have his right-hand man upon the earth performing miracles which make him appear to be a god. Referring to the Antichrist, the apostle says,

> Even him whose coming is after the working of Satan with all power and signs and lying wonders,

And with all deceivableness of unrighteousness in them that perish, because they received not the love of the truth, that they might be saved (2 Thess. 2:9, 10).

Inasmuch as we can expect an increase of open opposition to God on the part of the Satanic hordes, we who know Christ should humbly maintain fellowship with Him through full submission and ready obedience so that we may receive from Him the strength we need to overcome. James writes,

God resisteth the proud, but giveth grace unto the humble.
Submit yourselves, therefore, to God. Resist the devil, and he will flee from you (James 4: 6, 7).

Peter declares,

Be sober, be vigilant, because your adversary, the devil, like a roaring lion walketh about, seeking whom he may devour;
Whom resist steadfast in the faith, knowing that the same afflictions are accomplished in your brethren that are in the world (1 Pet. 5:8, 9).

No, Satan is not dead. He is like a wounded animal and still has great power to harm those who are careless or proud. Therefore, keep awake, be on the alert, read the Bible, and pray! If you don't, he may destroy your effectiveness as a Christian.

3

Satan and the World System

Are you aware that evil spirit beings operating through men in positions of authority and influence are the real motivators in human society? Yes, that is exactly what the Bible teaches! Perhaps this concept seems strange to you, almost like an outmoded superstition, but the Bible definitely states that Satan is the "god of this age" (2 Cor. 4:4), and that he is the leader of a well-organized army of beings invisible to men but very active among them. Paul tells us in Ephesians,

> For we wrestle not against flesh and blood, but against principalities, against powers, against the rulers of the darkness of this world, against spiritual wickedness in high places (Eph. 6:12).

These words indicate that evil spirits are organized into a military-like structure. The "principalities" are the highest ranking officers under Satan, the "powers" are officials of somewhat lower standing, and the "rulers of the darkness of this world" seem to be a special band of evil spirits whose sphere of influence includes the leaders of human government. The phrase "spiritual wickedness in high places" is better translated "spiritual hosts of wickedness in the heavenly places," and makes reference to the myriads of demonic hordes. They are all under the direction of Satan, who is not only named the "god of this age," but also is called "the prince of the power of the air" (Eph. 2:2).

I. The World System Defined

The Scriptures often speak of a close relationship between these evil spirits and the "world." In the Ephesians passage quoted above, you will remember that these spirit beings are called "the rulers of the darkness of this world." The apostle John also refers to the world, and it is significant that he considers it to be the Christian's enemy.

> Love not the world, neither the things that are in the world. If any man love the world, the love of the Father is not in him.
> For all that is in the world, the lust of the flesh, and the lust of the eyes, and the pride of life, is not of the Father, but is of the world.
> And the world passeth away, and the lust of it; but he that doeth the will of God abideth forever (1 John 2:15-17).

In addition, the same apostle declared that one who is "born of God overcometh *the world*" (1 John 5: 4), and also that "the whole *world* lieth in wickedness" (1 John 5:19). James, the brother of Jesus, declared in his epistle, "Whosoever therefore, will be a friend of the *world* is the enemy of God" (James 4:4). Before we can gain a full understanding of what this means, we must answer the following questions: What *is* this world, which if loved causes us to lose God's friendship? What *does* the Bible mean when it says that the whole world "lieth in wickedness"?

Certainly the Bible is not saying that Christians shouldn't love the world of nature, not is it implying that every person who isn't a Christian is an enemy to be overcome. In fact, the Scriptures often state that the glory of God is revealed in the natural world, and it specifically instructs believers not to antagonize other people, but to love them. No, the material universe in which we live is not opposed to us, and we are not to consider the people who inhabit the earth as our enemies.

The "world" referred to by John and James is the moral and spiritual system we call human society. Mankind, which has rejected God's revelation, has devised explanations of life, moral standards, and principles of conduct based upon human knowledge only. Man, on the whole, operates on erroneous principles, selfish desires, improper motives, and unworthy standards of value. The sciences, the arts, politics, and entertainment are all dominated by a humanistic approach to life which draws men away from God and makes man the "measure of all things."

II. THE CONTROL OF THE WORLD SYSTEM

The Bible teaches us that acceptance of this world system, influenced so strongly by Satan and his army of evil spirits, has caused men to adopt attitudes and to perform deeds which hinder God's work and harm His people. Society in every age is characterized by such iniquities as selfishness, pride, immorality, and dishonesty, in spite of the efforts of sincere people to make it a better world. Twentieth-century man, with more technical skill and knowledge than any previous generation, is unable to solve the problems of poverty, crime, racial hatred, and war. An increasing number of people go to bed hungry every night, crime is on the rise, racial hatred has never been more intense, and wars continue to be fought all over the world. Why? Because mankind has accepted a self-centered philosophy of life, and earth's citizens in general are motivated by the three evils of which John speaks in his first epistle — "the lust of the flesh, and the lust of the eyes, and the pride of life" (1 John 2:16).

The "lust of the flesh" is the desire for possession. It is the gratification of self by participation. Careful study of the word "flesh" indicates that this evil propensity of mankind involves more than just sins of impurity. The term, as used by John in this passage, does not have reference to the body but to the sinful Adamic nature. The individual sinner is born with a nature that is selfish, and he is part of a social structure which operates on grasping, egocentric, and selfish principles. A vast majority of men and women are materialistic, live to gratify the senses, and are self-centered even in the good things they do. Nations, too, seek only what is best for themselves. Leaders in industry, education, and even religion are primarily concerned about their own welfare, often neglecting the needs of those they serve. The "lust of the flesh" drives men and women to desire and obtain material possessions, and to satisfy their physical appetites and passions at the expense of spiritual values. This basic selfishness and craving for the earthly tangible pleasures of life leads people to misuse the physical and material blessings God has given all men to enjoy. On a worldwide scope, it has brought about a situation in which thousands live in unparalleled luxury while millions starve. When we stop to think about it, much of the world's unrest and unhappiness today can be traced to the "lust of the flesh."

The "lust of the eyes," the second characteristic of this world system, is sometimes defined as "gratification by contemplation." The use of our eyes has vast potential for either great blessing or for degradation. For example, we are able to look upon the endless beauty of creation and sing praises to the Lord. Reading God's Word, we can meditate upon the riches of glory in joyous expectation. But Satan and his evil partners have perverted the use of the eye, inducing wicked men to display scenes by which lustful thoughts are incited. They capitalize upon man's sinfulness and natural tendency to immorality. Down through the ages, immodest dress, impure books and pictures, and unholy theatrical productions have been used to degrade and degenerate both young and old. In addition, the eye affords an opportunity to enjoy by contemplation certain evils which one cannot or dare not actually perform. Therefore, people from all classes of society and every age bracket are influenced by the allurement that comes through the gift of sight. Discerning people who glance at the newsstands, read the advertisement in the theater page of the newspaper, or watch the programs and commercials presented on television, know full well that the "lust of the eyes" has been exploited by the powers of evil. The evidence certainly indicates that Satan and his followers are truly the "leaders of the darkness of this world."

The "pride of life," the third characteristic of this world system, refers to vanity and ostentation. Men and women put great stock in "being somebody." To make a name for themselves they throw impressive parties, purchase expensive automobiles, and live in luxurious homes. Their only measure of success is by these standards. Others may acquire academic degrees to display their intellectual prowess, while athletes may exert maximum effort, not principally out of team spirit, but for money and applause. The struggle for power, prestige, and even glory is at the heart of almost every human endeavor. But through all of this, mankind has been unable to discover true happiness and satisfaction. Most people confess they are not finding the pleasure they expected, but nonetheless continue on their way, ever pursuing new baubles. The invisible forces of Satan so blind men that they do not see true values, nor recognize the folly of their vain quest for this elusive will-o'-the-wisp, "the pride of life."

In summary, we must conclude that according to the Bible the whole social structure of this world is controlled by a pervading principle of life that is foreign to God and leads men away from Him. True, every man is a sinner by nature and alienated from God, but this inherent human selfishness, under the direction of intelligent and powerful wicked spirits, compounds this basic sinfulness by bringing out the very worst in men. Evil spirits cruelly blind and deceive fallen humanity through the lust of the flesh, the lust of the eyes, and the pride of life.

III. INFLUENCE OVER WORLD EVENTS

These fallen creatures actively try to manipulate the political rulers of the world. Satan's organized army operates quietly and invisibly in the minds and wills of earthly sovereigns to achieve their evil purposes. The Bible indicates the nature and course of their activity in several references.

Daniel 10 teaches that specific evil spirits are assigned the task of influencing human rulers. The chapter opens with a picture of Daniel in earnest prayer. He entreats the Lord for a period of three weeks, seeking God's favor upon the Jewish people who have returned to Jerusalem from captivity. He learned that they were experiencing difficulty in rebuilding the temple. Ezra 4, which gives the history of these former exiles, indicates that the work of restoration was interrupted by adversaries almost immediately after the foundation of the temple had been laid. Finally, three weeks after

Daniel began to pray, God sent him a most amazing experience. An angel came to Daniel and said,

> . . . Fear not, Daniel; for from the first day that thou didst set thine heart to understand, and to chasten thyself before thy God, thy words were heard, and I am come for thy words.
>
> But the prince of the kingdom of Persia withstood me one and twenty days; but, lo, Michael, one of the chief princes, came to help me; and I remained there with the kings of Persia (Dan. 10:12, 13).

The angel declared that he had left Heaven immediately after Daniel's first prayer, but that on his way to earth he had encountered opposition from "the prince of the kingdom of Persia." The heavenly messenger went on to say that it was not until Michael came to help him that he was able to overcome this opposing "prince." The struggle was obviously between angelic beings, for the one speaking to Daniel was an angel, and Michael is well known as the angelic protector of Israel. (See Dan. 10:21; 12:1; Jude 9; Rev. 12:7.) This "prince of the kingdom of Persia" was obviously a wicked spirit of high rank. He had been delegated by the arch-enemy of God, the devil himself, for the task of influencing the Persian government to obstruct the Israelites in their rebuilding program.

The success of this evil spirit's attempt was apparent upon earth. Even while the battle between the angelic beings was taking place in the air, the rulers of Persia were hindering the Jews in the task of rebuilding their temple. The people in Jerusalem could see only the treachery of their human enemies, not knowing that invisible spirits had been exerting pressure against them behind the scenes. The leaders of Persia were not aware that their decision to oppose Israel was the result of the working of evil spirits in their minds. These human rulers were actually mere puppets, carrying out the wishes of the invisible powers who were manipulating them.

Even today men who hold high political office may be the unwitting tools of evil spirits. Many men lust for power. National groups vie for supremacy in the economic world. In this prevailing atmosphere of selfishness, evil spirits are able to exert a great deal of influence upon men. Opportunistic politicians become ideal underlings of these evil spirits. In addition, the followers of Satan, in dominating the godless world rulers, are able to incite animal-like behavior in them. Many living today have witnessed the indescribable brutality of Nazism and atheistic Communism. Highly civilized people find great pleasure in the development of more effective weapons with which to kill members of other nations. Men tell lies, oppress others, and commit mass murders with no hint of shame or remorse. In fact, it is amazing that this modern age of civilization and refinement has been characterized by an inhumanity far worse than that of ancient barbaric times. We believe this pathological condition can be traced to the fact that many highly educated men of influence and power have rejected God. In so doing, they have opened themselves to the activity of evil spirits. Therefore, we have a confirmation of Paul's declaration that the real world rulers of this darkness (Eph. 6:12) are not the men who have positions of leadership, but the evil spirits who rule their hearts and influence their thoughts and decisions.

IV. LIMITATIONS OF SATANIC POWERS

It is reassuring, however, to know that the power of Satan and his hosts is limited by God's omnipotence. The Bible clearly teaches that the Lord is in ultimate control of the entire social and political realm. For example, in the story of Job, we are informed that Satan could do only what God allowed. The apostle Paul also tells us that the earthly rulers are in their places of authority by God's permissive decree. He declared,

> Let every soul be subject unto the higher powers. For there is no power but of God; the powers that be are ordained of God (Rom. 13:1).

This does not mean that God approves of men like Nero, Hitler, or Stalin, but that He ordained government to prevent chaos by making laws and enforcing them. Wicked men who hate the Lord and His people have obtained their positions of authority only by God's permission, and their power is limited by His will. Therefore, though He commands His followers to obey even the most evil of these earthly rulers, He will return as King of kings and Lord of lords to overcome all obstacles and work out His plans and purposes.

The power of Satan and his followers is further restricted by the presence of Christians in the world. Believers have been redeemed from the domination of this world system. In addition, obedient followers of the Lord Jesus exert a purifying and preserving influence in the world. Jesus said, "Ye are the salt of the earth" (Matt. 5:13). Salt immediately suggested purity to the people of Christ's day. In fact, the Romans said that salt was the purest of all things because it came from the sun and the sea. Believers in Christ, by holding to a high standard of speech and conduct, and keeping themselves "unspotted" from the world (James 1:27), exert a strong cleansing effect upon mankind. Then, too, as salt was a common preservative, so Christians are a cleansing antiseptic in society, holding back the process of corruption. Faithful believers in Christ are therefore both a purifying and preserving influence.

The apostle Paul also declared that all Christians are indwelt by the Holy Spirit, and that as long as they are on earth the full outbreak of evil is impossible.

> And now ye know what restraineth that he might be revealed in his time.
>
> For the mystery of iniquity doth already work; only he who now hindereth will continue to hinder until he be taken out of the way (2 Thess. 2:6, 7).

Moreover, Satan works under the handicap of knowing that his ultimate defeat has been made certain by the death and resurrection of Jesus Christ. The writer of Hebrews said that Jesus took upon Himself our nature and went to the cross that "through death he might destroy him that had the power of death, that is, the devil" (Heb. 2:14). Though Peter tells us that ". . . the devil, like a roaring lion walketh about, seeking whom he may devour" (1 Pet. 5:8), Satan knows his doom is sure and therefore operates under definite limitations.

In conclusion, if you are a follower of Christ, you must take seriously these Scripture passages which speak of the invisible army that is arrayed against you. You will not be victorious in your Christian life if you think that in your own strength you are able to withstand Satan and his hosts. Your testimony for Christ will be powerless and your way of life completely ineffective unless you walk in daily fellowship with God. This means you must confess and forsake every known sin, spend time with God in prayer, read the Scriptures, and submit yourself wholly to the Lord. In addition, believers are called upon to pray earnestly for the leaders of nations both on local and national levels. Remember, the Bible teaches that an invisible host of evil spirits often uses political leaders as mere pawns, and these men will not be able to function effectively and promote the right unless they receive help from the Lord. Since many of them are not true believers, they especially stand in need of the prayers of God's people. The experience of Daniel demonstrates that when godly men pray, the Lord sends His holy angels to do battle with the Satanic forces and frustrates them in their efforts. Christians are therefore reminded by Paul to pray for all who have positions of authority:

> I exhort, therefore, that first of all, supplications, prayers, intercessions, and giving of thanks, be made for all men,
> For kings, and for all that are in authority, that we may lead a quiet and peaceable life in all godliness and honesty (1 Tim. 2:1, 2).

Many of God's people do not realize the tremendous battle being waged in the spiritual realm, and as a result they are somewhat lackadaisical about praying for men and women who hold responsible positions in government. Therefore, we who know that evil spirits are putting tremendous pressure upon these people should make doubly sure we do not fail. Our prayers may make the difference between life or death for many people, for when we seek God's face, He exerts His power to defeat the enemy.

4

Satan and Spiritism

Spiritism is the belief that people survive death as spirits, and that they can communicate with the living through a medium, a person having a special psychic gift. The fact has been established that nearly 100 million people in the world today have participated with some regularity in efforts to receive messages from the dead. Many have had experiences so convincing that they now possess unwavering assurance of a future existence in another world after death.

One such man was the late Bishop Pike, a liberal theologian who at one time did not believe any form of life was possible on the other side of the grave. But then a series of strange circumstances impelled him to go to a medium, who claimed to be able to put him in touch with his dead son Jim. The young man had recently committed suicide, and the bishop left the seance satisfied that Jim had really spoken to him through the medium. In fact, he was persuaded that he had also conversed with the late Dr. Paul Tillich, a celebrated theologian and philosopher whom the bishop had greatly admired and to whom he had dedicated one of his books.

Dr. Pike, with Diane Kennedy who later became his wife, published a book entitled *The Other Side,* in which they told the whole story of his spirit encounters, beginning with the haunted apartment in Cambridge, England, and including his seances with Ena Twigg, George Daisley, and Arthur Ford.

A number of the events recounted are so extraordinary that they baffle the mind. One cannot read this book without concluding that Bishop Pike was either the victim of a plot so carefully contrived that no one to this date has been able to decipher it, or that he actually participated in some kind of supernatural activity. In any case, we do not agree with the bishop's assumption that he had spoken with his son or with Dr. Tillich.

Many people have written recently of their experiences in spiritism, and some of them come to conclusions far different from those of Bishop Pike and his associates. Raphael Gasson, a former medium who was converted to Christ, recently published a work entitled *The Challenging Counterfeit.* He convincingly sets forth the idea that demons, by impersonating the dead, are able to deceive those who attend seances in hope of contacting the spirits of their loved ones. In another publication, *I Talked With Spirits,* Victor Ernest tells the story of his early life as a member of a spiritualistic family. He is now a highly respected minister of the Gospel, and declares unequivocally that the religion of his childhood contained supernatural elements, but that it is dangerous and wicked.

In this study we will carefully examine spiritism, seeking to answer four basic questions: (1) What does the Bible teach regarding spiritism? (2) How do spiritists work? (3) What do spiritists believe? (4) Why is spiritism dangerous?

I. Biblical Teaching About Spiritism

The Word of God clearly and emphatically condemns all efforts to communicate with the dead. The Lord declares that the observances of people who engage in such activity are equivalent to the worship of other gods.

> Regard not them that have familiar spirits, neither seek after wizards, to be defiled by them: I am the LORD your God (Lev. 19:31).

The Lord indicated that this practice was one of the factors that contributed to the moral and spiritual corruption of the Canaanites.

> When thou art come into the land which the LORD thy God giveth thee, thou shalt not learn to do after the abominations of those nations.
>
> There shall not be found among you anyone who maketh his son or his daughter pass through the fire, or who useth divination, or an observer of times, or an enchanter, or a witch,
>
> Or a charmer, or a consultor of mediums, or a wizard, or a necromancer (Deut. 18:9-11).

Anyone in Israel who served as a medium or engaged in sorcery was to be put to death. The fact that such a severe penalty was imposed is the Divine testimony to the supernatural, destructive, and demoralizing nature of spiritism.

> A man also or woman who hath a familiar spirit, or who is a wizard, shall surely be put to death: they shall stone them with stones; their blood shall be upon them (Lev. 20:27).

These verses from the Old Testament should be sufficient to convince everyone who professes to believe the Bible that all efforts to communicate with the dead are forbidden by God. The person who has read them and still consults mediums to make contact with the spirit of someone who has died is guilty of deliberate disobedience. God will not allow any believer to engage in this sin with impunity.

The story of Saul and the witch of Endor often has been cited as a Biblical example of actual communication with the dead through a medium. Spiritists have contended that since Israel's first king actually talked with the spirit of the departed Samuel, one cannot deny the possibility of communicating with those who have died. But a careful study of the account shows that God, not the medium, really brought Samuel from the realm of the dead. Here is the Biblical record:

> Then said Saul unto his servants, Seek me a woman who is a medium, that I may go to her, and inquire of her. And his servants said to him, Behold, there is a woman who is a medium at Endor.
>
> And Saul disguised himself, and put on other raiment, and he went, and two men with him, and they came to the woman by night; and he said, I pray thee, divine unto me as a medium, and bring me him up, whom I shall name unto thee.
>
> And the woman said unto him, Behold, thou knowest what Saul hath done, how he hath cut off those who are mediums, and the wizards, out of the land. Why, then, layest thou a snare for my life, to cause me to die?
>
> And Saul swore to her by the LORD, saying, As the LORD liveth, there shall no punishment happen to thee for this thing.
>
> Then said the woman, Whom shall I bring up unto thee? And he said, Bring me up Samuel.
>
> And when the woman saw Samuel, she cried with a loud voice. And the woman spoke to Saul, saying, Why hast thou deceived me? For thou art Saul.
>
> And the king said unto her, Be not afraid; for what sawest thou? And the woman said unto Saul, I saw gods ascending out of the earth.
>
> And he said unto her, What form is he of? And she said, An old man cometh up, and he is covered with a mantle. And Saul perceived that it was Samuel, and he stooped with his face to the ground, and bowed himself.
>
> And Samuel said to Saul, Why hast thou disquieted me, to bring me up? And Saul answered, I am very much distressed; for the Philistines make war against me, and God is departed from

me and answereth me no more, neither by prophets, nor by dreams; therefore, I have called
thee, that thou mayest make known unto me
what I shall do.

Then said Samuel, Why, then, dost thou ask
of me, seeing the LORD is departed from thee,
and is become thine enemy?

And the LORD hath done to thee, as he spoke
by me; for the LORD hath torn the kingdom out
of thine hand, and given it to thy neighbor, even
to David.

Because thou obeyedst not the voice of the
LORD, nor executedst his fierce wrath upon Ama-
lek. Therefore hath the LORD done this thing
unto thee this day.

Moreover, the LORD will also deliver Israel
with thee into the hand of the Philistines, and
tomorrow shalt thou and thy sons be with me.
The LORD also shall deliver the host of Israel
into the hand of the Philistines.

Then Saul fell immediately full length on the
earth, and was very much afraid, because of the
words of Samuel; and there was no strength in
him; for he had eaten no bread all the day, nor
all the night.

And the woman came unto Saul, and saw that
he was very much troubled, and said unto him,
Behold, thine handmaid hath obeyed thy voice,
and I have put my life in my hand, and have
hearkened unto thy words which thou didst speak
unto me.

Now, therefore, I pray thee, hearken thou also
unto the voice of thine handmaid, and let me set
a morsel of bread before thee; and eat, that thou
mayest have strength, when thou goest on thy
way.

But he refused, and said, I will not eat. But
his servants, together with the woman, compelled
him; and he hearkeneth unto their voice. So he
arose from the earth, and sat upon the bed.

And the woman had a fat calf in the house;
and she hastened and killed it, and took flour,
and kneaded it, and baked unleavened bread of
it;

And she brought it before Saul, and before his servants, and they did eat. Then they rose up, and went away that night (1 Sam. 28:7-25).

We see God's power at work in spite of the action of the medium, not because of her incantations, for the following reasons: First, the spirit of Samuel actually left the realm of the dead and spoke to Saul. The king never doubted that the form which appeared and the voice he heard belonged to Samuel, God's faithful servant. Second, the message spoken by the spirit was true. It contained a rebuke to Saul for his disobedience in failing to destroy the Amalekites as God had commanded. (See 1 Sam. 15:1-31.) It was a declaration of judgment, emphatically stating that the Lord had departed from Saul and become his enemy. It was also a true prophecy, for it said that Saul and his sons would die the next day, and the prediction was literally fulfilled. Yes, there is no doubt the message came from Samuel. Third, we do not believe that the witch was responsible for bringing his spirit from the realm of the dead, because she screamed in terror when she saw the spirit of Samuel. She was either a fraud, able to deceive people into thinking she received messages from the other side, or a genuine medium with the ability to make contact with demons. In the latter case, she would have expected a demon to impersonate Samuel. That is why she was surprised and frightened when the actual spirit of Samuel miraculously made its appearance.

God was displeased that King Saul sought help from the witch of Endor. Notice what the writer of 1 Chronicles says.

So Saul died for his transgression which he committed against the LORD, even against the word of the LORD, which he kept not, and also for asking counsel of a medium, to inquire of her,

And inquired not of the LORD; therefore, he slew him, and turned the kingdom unto David, the son of Jesse (1 Chron. 10:13, 14).

This text states that these two sins of Saul brought about his death at the hand of the Philistines. First, the king had transgressed against the Lord through an act of disobedience. (See 1 Sam. 13:8-14 and 15:12-23.) Second, he sinned grievously by going to a medium instead of returning to the Lord in humble and penitent prayer. In fact, King Saul's visit to the necromancer was the crowning sin of his troubled life.

Though the New Testament does not specifically repeat the warnings against consulting mediums, it clearly teaches the existence of demons and the reality of a world of evil spirits under the direction of Satan. We have no reason for thinking that necromancy today is less dangerous or offensive to God than in the past, and we therefore must heed the Old Testament prohibitions. The Lord Jesus confirmed the Old Testament teaching that the dead cannot really send messages to the living and also showed that no need for communication with those who have died exists. In His story of the rich man and Lazarus, He portrayed Abraham as declaring first that the gulf between the saved and unsaved in the spirit world is impassable, and then as denying the rich man's request that someone from the realm of the dead warn his living brothers. The patriarch said that people on earth have the Scriptures, and added, "If they hear not Moses and the prophets, neither will they be persuaded, though one rose from the dead" (Luke 16:31).

In summary, the Scriptures never once indicate the possibility of actually receiving messages from the dead through a medium. Jesus also declared that such communication with the spirits of those who have died would have no eternal value, for such conversations between citizens of two worlds would not lead the living to faith in Christ. Then, too, the Old Testament Scriptures which unequivocally condemn all such effort are still in force today. We therefore conclude that Bishop Pike never really conversed with his dead son. He was either the victim of a carefully and skillfully contrived plot on the part of an international group of mediums, or he spoke with a demon who impersonated the voice and mannerisms of his son. Believers should consider all forms of necromancy to be both unnecessary and sinful. The mediums who purportedly make contact with the spirit world are either quacks, deliberately deceiving their victims, or emissaries of Satan, somehow placed in touch with members of the devil's invisible army.

II. The Methods of Spiritism

When an individual seeks a message from the spirit of someone who has died, he almost always goes to a medium. Such a person possesses an unusual amount of psychic ability, supposedly enabling him to make contact with the spirit world. These people are sometimes called necromancers, and often are able to put on bizarre and frightening displays as proof of their psychic power. They may cause objects or people to float in the air, produce music from a piano that no one is touching, or cause a horn to blow which appears to be miraculously suspended and moving about the room. Some of these phenomena undoubtedly are accomplished by clever mechanical means as the work of impostors, but in some instances scientific men have discerned no evidence of human manipulation. This has caused a number of atheists and agnostics, after conducting extensive investigations, to speak vaguely of a non-material and indefinable spiritual power in the universe with which certain psychic individuals can relate. Christians, on the other hand, know that the phenomena we have been speaking about may at least in part be attributed to the activity of the invisible spirit world, which the Bible depicts as being under Satan's control.

When a medium is called upon to relay a message which supposedly comes from the realm of the dead, he usually goes into a trance. This is a state which *Webster's New World Dictionary* defines as "a condition in which a spiritualist medium allegedly loses consciousness and passes under the control of some external force, as for the supposed transmission of communications from the dead." In a state of unconsciousness, the necromancer may obtain communication in the form of automatic writing, but it usually comes through verbal speech. Sometimes the phenomenon called "materialization" occurs. This is defined as the ability on the part of some mediums "to create from unknown materials outside of their own body, some visible, tangible, more or less highly organized new formations supplied with their own illumination (such as efflorescent substance) for which formations in many cases, the human body in part or in whole forms a pattern, and these materializations appear and disappear suddenly" (Kurt Koch, *Christian Counseling and Occultism,* p. 137, quoting from Professor Gruber). Many reputable writers report that the materializations actually have been photographed and carefully studied. They are sometimes called phantasms, and seem to speak while the medium appears to be unconscious.

When a materialization does not occur, the unconscious medium often speaks in a voice that sounds exactly like that of the deceased person he has been attempting to reach. Many people have gone to a seance believing the whole idea to be fraudulent, but have become firmly convinced that they truly heard a loved one who had died.

Automatic writing is another baffling spiritistic marvel. The mediums may, while in a trance, inscribe a paper with the exact handwriting of the deceased. At other times a pencil may write without being touched by the human hand or any apparent mechanical device. Then again, in some instances a phantasm does the transcribing.

Of course, before we accept reports of this nature, we must recognize the possibilities of deliberate deceit, overwrought imagination, or inaccurate observation. On the other hand, one is not being fair if he simply dismisses the testimony of intelligent, honest, God-fearing men as having no value. A further word of caution is in order. Christians may be tempted to conclude that these strange and unexplainable phenomena are proofs of God's existence. This is not correct because many of them may have a naturalistic explanation. Writings produced mysteriously in seances have been carefully examined by graphologists, and have even become the objects over which court battles have been fought.

If one is interested in studying multiplied accounts of automatic writings and other such phenomena, he may do so by reading *Between Christ and Satan* by Dr. Kurt Koch, *I Talked With Spirits* by Victor Ernest, and *Demons in the World Today* by Dr. Merrill F. Unger.

To summarize, spiritists usually attempt their alleged contact with the spirit world through a medium who enters what appears to be a trance, and receives some kind of communication in either verbal or written form. Undoubtedly some people who claim to have this ability are impostors, but hundreds of educated men who have been closely involved in this activity or have conducted intensive investigations are convinced that extraordinary, perhaps supernatural, spiritual power is involved. But we who believe the Bible are certain that all necromancy is sinful and dangerous.

III. What Spiritualists and Spiritists Believe

In discussing the religious beliefs of people who seek to converse with the dead, we can distinguish between those who claim to be "Christian" and those who make no pretense of accepting historic Christianity. The distinction between these groups is sometimes made by using the term "spiritualist" to denote the ones who profess to believe the Bible, and designating the others as "spiritists."

Those we have called spiritualists often open their meetings with prayer, the singing of hymns, and the reading of the Scriptures. They teach the golden rule as the standard by which people should live, and some of them revere Jesus as the greatest of all mediums. They conceive of God as primarily a universal force, and place little emphasis upon His personality. Their doctrine of the after-life is a curious mixture of ideas that come from Hinduism, Buddhism, Theosophy, and other religions, and bears almost no resemblance to the teaching of the Bible. They deny Hell and look upon Heaven as a series of spiritual planes through which the souls of the dead pass in an evolutionary process. Those who live most wickedly begin on the very lowest plane, and need a great deal of help from other spirits to advance to the next sphere. The individual who does not smoke, nor drink alcoholic beverages, is kind, honest, and lives a clean moral life, will begin on a higher plane than one who is intemperate or immoral.

While some of these teachings are commendable, spiritualism is clearly a false system. It does not confess that Jesus Christ is the second Person of the Trinity, nor does it accept His sin-atoning death or physical resurrection. It is therefore guilty of denying the very heart of the Gospel of God's grace, and does not by any stretch of the imagination deserve to be called "Christian."

The second group, the spiritists, attempt to communicate with the dead without any distinct reference to the Christian faith. They are to be commended for their honesty, for they do not try to give their practices a superficial religious window-dressing. They usually admit that they cannot understand what happens in their seances. They believe that certain psychically gifted people possess the power to exert an invisible and incomprehensible force through which they can contact the spirits of the dead. Though totally naturalistic, some even atheistic, they still believe in continued existence after death.

The spiritualists, the first group mentioned, are the most dangerous, because they are more likely to deceive uninstructed believers. These so-called Christians say they believe the Bible, speak well of Jesus, and set forth high standards of ethics and morals. They may even call Jesus their Savior, and the Son of God, but their concept of salvation and of Christ is far from Scriptural. The devil, using every device imaginable to deceive believers and confuse unsaved people, often mixes truth and error to accomplish his ends. Paul warned the Christians in Corinth about false teachers who called themselves apostles of Christ, but were actually deceitful workers teaching error. He added,

> And no marvel; for Satan himself is transformed into an angel of light.
> Therefore, it is no great thing if his ministers also be transformed as the ministers of righteousness, whose end shall be according to their works (2 Cor. 11:14, 15).

The archenemy of God will advocate an upright moral life if by this means he can deceive sincere people into seeking salvation by works instead of through faith in Jesus Christ. Christians must therefore reject without qualification the teachings of those who hold seances and try to communicate with the spirits of the dead. Spiritualism, even when dressed in Biblical garb, is not true Christianity.

IV. WHY IS NECROMANCY DANGEROUS?

Every believer in the Lord Jesus must consider spiritism in all of its forms to be a grave danger, and he should strictly avoid it. He must obey without question the many Biblical prohibitions of necromancy. A Christian who becomes involved in this kind of activity will bring harm to himself and/or others. He should also warn unsaved friends and relatives, realizing they will become increasingly difficult to reach for Christ if they become enslaved by the powers of evil that are part and parcel of spiritism.

You see, the Lord doesn't look upon dabbling in occultism as merely being deceived or cheated by a group of charlatans. A real power of Satan is at work in various forms of spiritism. Under our first heading in this chapter we quoted a number of

Scriptures which show that God demanded the death penalty for necromancers, and the consulting of a medium was considered the same as seeking help from a false god. The power of Satan in heathenism is indicated by the fact that its leaders sometimes exercised supernatural powers. For example, the Egyptian sorcerers were able to duplicate some of the miracles of judgment wrought by Aaron and Moses. (See Exod. 7 - 8:19.)

It is well to bear in mind that the heathen idols, though nothing but wood, stone, or metal in themselves, were the props by which men and women actually worshiped demons. This affirmation is clearly set forth in Paul's letter to the Christians in Corinth. He told them that he recognized an idol in itself to be nothing, and that if they unknowingly ate food which the heathen had dedicated to an imaginary god, they would be doing no harm to themselves or anyone else. He went on to say, however, that they should not participate with pagans in their sacrificial festivals, for behind the whole system of idolatry was the kingdom of darkness. Though the heathen did not realize it, they were actually presenting offerings to the world of evil spirits. Therefore, Paul wrote,

> Behold Israel after the flesh. Are not they who eat of the sacrifices partakers of the altar?
> What say I, then? That the idol is anything, or that which is offered in sacrifices to idols is anything?
> But I say that the things which the Gentiles sacrifice, they sacrifice to demons, and not to God; and I would not that ye should have fellowship with demons.
> Ye cannot drink the cup of the Lord, and the cup of demons; ye cannot be partakers of the Lord's table, and of the table of demons (1 Cor. 10:18-21).

In a very real sense, the person who tries to communicate with the dead through a medium is eating at "the table of demons." By doing this he is repudiating "the Lord's table," for all the precious truths symbolized in the Lord's Supper are denied by the spiritualists. Therefore, if a believer becomes involved in spiritism and then partakes of the Lord's Supper, he is flagrantly disobeying the Scriptures and will be severely chastened. He has participated in the Lord's Supper unworthily, that is, in an unworthy manner, and the apostle warned,

> Wherefore, whosoever shall eat this bread, and drink this cup of the Lord, unworthily, shall be guilty of the body and blood of the Lord.
> But let a man examine himself, and so let him eat of that bread, and drink of that cup.
> For he that eateth and drinketh unworthily, eateth and drinketh judgment to himself, not discerning the Lord's body.
> For this cause many are weak, and sickly among you, and many sleep (1 Cor. 11:27-30).

In addition to making oneself subject to divine chastening, the Christian who disobeys God's warning against necromancy may experience deep depression, the inability to pray, the loss of interest in the Bible, and a compulsive desire to engage in sins which formerly repulsed him. Missionaries and Christian workers from all over the world testify that they can often link deep spiritual depression, disturbing delusions, or paralyzing fears with an incident in which the patient or counselee attended a seance or engaged in some form of occultism.

Dr. Alfred Lechler, who for thirty-five years served as the medical superintendent of the largest mental hospital in Germany, definitely believes that even today Satan manifests himself in supernatural ways when Christians tamper with the occult. The Swiss author and physician, Dr. Paul Tournier, also believes in the reality of demonic oppression as the result of disobedience to God in these matters. Dr. William S. Reed, a well-known Christian psychiatrist, declared, "Many mental and physical illnesses result, in fact, from demonic attacks. Exorcism must therefore be given a place in present-day psychiatry and medicine." I am pointing this out to impress upon everyone who reads this book that the Biblical warnings against spiritism must be taken seriously by every Christian.

It is interesting to note that true believers in Christ are especially vulnerable to Satanic attack when they attend a seance or engage in some form of occultism. Dr. Unger, in *Demons in the World Today,* declares it to be a well-documented fact that adherents of Buddhism, Islam, or even false cults of Christianity sense little or no ill effects from their contact with mediums. Apparently Satan is pleased whenever someone adopts spiritism in any of its forms as his religion. Let every true believer take heed! Never, never engage in any practice by which efforts are made to contact the spirits of the dead!

5

Satan and Fortunetelling

Human beings are subject to special tensions just because they, unlike animals, have been endowed with the ability to reflect upon themselves and their future. The cow that lies in a rich pasture blissfully chewing her cud is perfectly content and free from care, but men and women find themselves worrying about tomorrow, next year, the years after that, and even about death and eternity. Many people don't like to be engrossed in this kind of reflection; but even though they seek to exclude such ruminations by busying themselves in one way or another, they cannot keep disquieting thoughts from haunting them from time to time.

When a person becomes a Christian and lives in fellowship with God, however, he doesn't have to dodge the sobering realities of life and death. He can reflect upon the future without becoming depressed or fearful. He can talk about death, either his own or that of a loved one, without being engulfed by morbid feelings. He can face the possibility of nuclear war and worldwide destruction without despairing. Why? Because he believes in an all-powerful, all-knowing, and all-loving God. He is assured that Jesus Christ paid the price for his sin on Calvary, and is confident that the power of death has been destroyed by Christ's resurrection. Believing that a glorious eternity awaits him in Heaven, he isn't afraid to die. For these reasons, he doesn't need a fortuneteller to analyze cards, read his palm, or gaze into a crystal ball. Nor does he have to consult the horoscope for information and advice. He places no confidence in the visions of self-styled prophets. Instead, he reads the Bible to find God's message of instruction and comfort, and through prayer he receives the strength and grace he needs day by day.

Most people, either through ignorance or determined unbelief, have never placed their trust in Christ. In fact, multitudes have more or less ruled out the idea of God from their thinking, and therefore possess no real hope for the future. This attitude of unbelief may suffice for some people part of the time, but the uncertainties, problems, disappointments, and sorrows of life are so great that many must look somewhere beyond themselves for help. A large percentage of such people in recent years have turned to occultism, and claim to have found a measure of satisfaction in it.

We pointed out earlier that an ever-increasing number of people are visiting mediums to make contact with the spirits of loved ones who have died, and think they have succeeded in communicating with them. We also mentioned that Bishop James A. Pike actually came to believe in life after death through the seances in which he allegedly spoke to his son Jim. This is certainly a poor basis for confidence in continued existence on the other side of the grave, but, sad to say, many people anchor their hope for eternity upon such experiences.

We find it very disturbing that the whole field of occultic activity is gaining in popularity. Some of the most influential people in the world today, including prime ministers and presidents, military leaders, congressmen, and high-salaried businessmen, regularly consult mystics and those who purport to have psychic powers. These fortunetellers claim they can predict the future through astrology, the use of tarot cards, the crystal ball, or other devices. In fact, law enforcement agencies in seventeen countries have called in Peter Hurkoes, who is reputed to possess unusual psychic power, to help solve murder cases. Respected magazines like *Business Week* and *Time* have featured articles in which they discuss seriously some of the amazing and unexplained phenomena of the occultic world. The prophecies of Jeane Dixon have received wide acclaim, and her biography, written by Ruth Montgomery, has been purchased by millions. When one looks at the book section of any store selling paperbacks, he cannot help but be amazed by the large number of volumes devoted to fortunetelling and other occultic activities. Horoscopes are included in thousands of newspapers and magazines, and the selling of occultic materials and related enterprises is indeed a rapidly growing and highly lucrative business.

The two main sources of information about the future are the alleged visions of people who call themselves prophets and the prognostications that come from astrology.

I. Prophetic Visions

The public today is not surprised when someone talks about "the gift of prophecy." Even among those who have had little or no contact with the Bible are many who maintain that certain people are able to foretell the future. This is an amazing and paradoxical phenomenon of our scientific age. True, self-styled prophets and fortunetellers have appeared in every generation, but usually little attention has been paid them by most people. Today, however, millions of intelligent and well-educated members of our affluent society are spending vast sums of money for books, magazines, and private consultations to gain information about the future.

A person who has only a superficial knowledge of what the Bible teaches may be inclined to think that anyone who claims to have the gift of prophecy and speaks well of God and Christ is to be considered genuine and trustworthy. Nothing could be farther from the truth! An individual may live an outwardly respectable life, teach a noble system of ethics, and speak of Jesus Christ in a highly complimentary manner, but still be a servant of the forces of evil. Remember, Paul warned believers that the devil is so clever he will make himself and his followers appear as "angels of light," if necessary, to deceive people who are not well-grounded in the faith.

> For such are false apostles, deceitful workers, transforming themselves into the apostles of Christ.
> And no marvel; for Satan himself is transformed into an angel of light.
> Therefore, it is no great thing if his ministers also be transformed as the ministers of righteousness, whose end shall be according to their works (2 Cor. 11:13-15).

Believers must carefully examine the life and doctrine of any person who claims the gift of prophecy, and use Scriptural principles to make an accurate evaluation.

Let us turn the searchlight on Mrs. Dixon, perhaps the best-known fortuneteller of today. She is reported to be a very religious person who advocates and lives a highly moral life. She has recorded a number of her alleged visions, consults an old deck of cards given her by a gypsy lady, gazes into a crystal ball, writes horoscopes, and has made numerous specific prophecies. She gained her reputation as a prophetess because of an unusual number of accurate predictions. She foretold the death of President Franklin Roosevelt, and predicted Harry Truman's election defeat of Thomas Dewey. She also stated that the communists would obtain control of China long before the takeover actually occurred, and foresaw the coming to power of Nikita Khrushchev, his removal from office, and the orbiting of Sputnik. In addition, she warned that an assassination attempt would be made upon President John F. Kennedy in Dallas. Strangely enough, she even gives advice to men who bet on horse races and predicts the success or failure of certain business enterprises. Some astute gamblers and businessmen claim her predictive "batting average" is so high they consider her a genuine mystic.

But does this mean she is really endowed with the "gift of prophecy" of which the Bible speaks? We say, "No!" And we will give Biblical reasons for this positive declaration.

In the first place, she is not batting a thousand, which is required if one is to be considered a genuine prophet of God. The Almighty never makes mistakes. In the Old Testament He told the Israelites that they were to test the validity of a person's claim to be a prophet by the accuracy of his predictions. No one was to be considered God's spokesman unless what he said concerning the near future actually came to pass in every detail. As you read the Old Testament, you will notice that the prophets never spoke only of events far in the future. They always preached a message relevant to their own day, and included prophecies of things which would soon take place. If these predictions were not fulfilled in every respect, the spokesman was not to be accepted as a prophet of God.

And if thou say in thine heart, How shall we know the word which the LORD hath not spoken?

> When a prophet speaketh in the name of the
> Lord, if the thing follow not, nor come to pass,
> that is the thing which the Lord hath not spoken,
> but the prophet hath spoken it presumptuously;
> thou shalt not be afraid of him (Deut. 18:21,
> 22).

Mrs. Dixon has not maintained a perfect "batting average." She may be hitting a little better than .500, but this is not high enough. For example, she prophesied peace in Vietnam as far back as 1965, said that Richard Nixon would defeat John F. Kennedy in the 1960 presidential election, and declared that Walter Reuther would run for the presidency in 1964.

No other present-day fortuneteller does any better. Therefore, not one of them is qualified to be considered as an inspired prophet of God. In addition, any person who dabbles in occult activity forfeits the right to be God's spokesman. That the Lord strongly forbade such practices cannot be questioned. Listen to the words of Isaiah:

> Therefore shall evil come upon thee; thou shalt
> not know from where it riseth, and mischief shall
> fall upon thee; thou shalt not be able to put it
> off, and desolation shall come upon thee sud-
> denly, which thou shalt not know.
> Stand now with thine enchantments, and with
> the multitude of thy sorceries, in which thou hast
> labored from thy youth, if so be thou mayest
> prevail.
> Thou art wearied in the multitude of thy coun-
> sels. Let now the astrologers, the stargazers, the
> monthly prognosticators, stand up, and save thee
> from these things that shall come upon thee.
> Behold, they shall be like stubble; the fire
> shall burn them; they shall not deliver themselves
> from the power of the flame; there shall not be a
> coal to warm at, nor fire to sit before it.
> Thus shall they be unto thee with whom thou
> hast labored, even thy merchants, from thy youth;

they shall wander every one to his quarter; none shall save thee (Isa. 47:11-15).

Anyone who disobeys these clear prohibitions cannot be a prophet for God.

Another reason to avoid present-day fortune-tellers is that their visions and messages often do not square with the teachings of the Bible. Their unbiblical statements are serious, for they claim to speak by direct communication from God. The Bible teacher who makes errors in his interpretation of certain Scriptures can admit his blunders without embarrassment because he does not claim infallibility. A prophet, however, should never err, for the very nature of his message as coming directly from the Lord would implicate the Almighty, not the human instrument. Since Mrs. Dixon is regarded as a prophet, not a Biblical student, her errors are of a different nature than the ones preachers sometimes make. And she does blunder occasionally! For example, in her description of her first vision, which allegedly took place on July 14, 1952, she said that a huge serpent approached her bed and slowly entwined itself around her body. As she looked into the eyes of this creature, she saw that they were full of love, goodness, and knowledge, and a deep sense of peace flowed through her.

Anyone well-versed in the Scriptures cannot help but be puzzled by this strange interpretation of the serpent's significance. Mrs. Dixon made it represent goodness, knowledge, peace, and love, but this is in direct contradiction to the consistent Biblical symbolism of the serpent. All through the Bible it is associated with Satan and sin.

The instructed Bible student also raises serious questions when he studies Mrs. Dixon's interpretation of a vision she claims to have received on

February 5, 1962. This happened to be a day when an unusual conjunction of the planets occurred, and astrologers were unanimous in declaring that a significant event would take place on that date. Mrs. Dixon reports that the lights in her house began to flicker, first dimming and then burning brightly. She went to bed, and awakened before sunrise. She looked out her window toward the east, and in vision saw an Egyptian pharaoh with his queen Nefertiti walking toward her on the rays of the sun. Both the king and queen were gorgeously attired in royal apparel, but the wife was holding in her arms an infant dressed in rags. Mrs. Dixon said that when she looked into the eyes of the baby, she saw that they were full of wisdom. Then, as she continued to gaze at the scene, she saw the baby grow into manhood, and, to her amazement, a small cross which was suspended over his head became larger and larger until it stretched over the entire earth. Soon people from every part of the world knelt before this man in adoring worship.

This so-called vision, considered by itself, could be quite naturally explained. It contained elements Mrs. Dixon could have drawn easily from reading the Bible and other books on ancient history, and one might believe that she was actually asleep and dreaming instead of awake and beholding a vision. The astonishing element in the whole story is the fact that Mrs. Dixon has set forth two conflicting interpretations of what the vision meant.

In her first report she said that the baby who became a man and was worshiped represented the great leader of a new Christianity, and predicted that he would unite the people of every sect and creed in the service of God. She declared that a baby, born somewhere in the Middle East shortly after 7 A.M. E.S.T. on 5 February 1962, is the world's great hope. He will be the founder of this new and perfect form of the Christian faith.

Her explanation of the meaning of this vision was a surprise to devout Bible scholars. Anyone who is familiar with the prophetic Scriptures knows that the Bible does not predict the coming of a second christ to perfect the Christian faith. In fact, it declares unequivocally that a great enemy of the Lord Jesus will make his appearance, and that he is the Antichrist. The apostle John declared,

> Little children, it is the last time; and as ye have heard that antichrist shall come, even now are there many antichrists, by which we know that it is the last time (1 John 2:18).

Every enemy of Christ (*antichristos*) and every self-styled christ (*pseudo christos*) who have crossed the threshold of history are forerunners in miniature of the one exceedingly powerful and indescribable wicked man who will be "the Antichrist." In the book of Revelation, the beloved apostle portrays a seven-headed beast who rises from the sea and swiftly becomes the world dictator. His coming up out of the water symbolizes that his rise to power will take place in the midst of turbulent conditions among the nations, and the fact that he is closely related to the dragon (Satan) reveals immediately his true character. He is a blasphemer, world ruler, and along with Satan becomes the object of human worship. In fact, he demands that people revere him as God, and instigates bitter persecution against those who refuse to bow down to him. Here are the words of John:

> And I stood upon the sand of the sea, and saw a beast rise up out of the sea, having seven heads

and ten horns, and upon his horns ten crowns, and upon his heads the name of blasphemy.

And the beast which I saw was like a leopard, and his feet were like the feet of a bear, and his mouth like the mouth of a lion; and the dragon gave him his power, and his throne, and great authority.

And I saw one of his heads as though it were wounded to death; and his deadly wound was healed, and all the world wondered after the beast.

And they worshiped the dragon who gave power unto the beast; and they worshiped the beast, saying, Who is like the beast? Who is able to make war with him?

And there was given unto him a mouth speaking great things and blasphemies, and power was given unto him to continue forty and two months.

And he opened his mouth in blasphemy against God, to blaspheme his name, and his tabernacle, and them that dwell in heaven.

And it was given unto him to make war with the saints, and to overcome them; and power was given him over all kindreds, and tongues, and nations.

And all that dwell upon the earth shall worship him, whose names are not written in the book of life of the Lamb slain from the foundation of the world.

If any man have an ear, let him hear.

He that leadeth into captivity shall go into captivity; he that killeth with the sword must be killed with the sword. Here is the patience and the faith of the saints (Rev. 13:1-10).

This same enemy of Christ is presented in the Old Testament Scriptures. Daniel refers to him as the willful king who rises to power, blasphemes the Almighty, and magnifies himself as God. (See Dan. 11:36-45.) The apostle Paul spoke of him in 2 Thessalonians, referring to him as the man of sin, the son of perdition, that wicked one, and "him whose coming is after the working of Satan with all power and signs and lying wonders, and with all deceivableness of unrighteousness in them that perish, because they received not the love of the truth, that they might be saved." (See 2 Thess. 2:1-12.)

In the light of these Scriptures, it seems that the baby of Mrs. Dixon's alleged vision should represent the Antichrist rather than the founder of a "new Christianity." Apparently Jeane Dixon had second thoughts too, for she changed her mind. We find ourselves wondering what happened. Did she restudy the Bible? Or was she influenced by the literature of some scholar? At any rate, on page 203 of her second book, entitled *My Life and Prophecies* (1969) she wrote, "There is no doubt in my mind that the 'child' is the actual person of the Antichrist, the one who will deceive the world in Satan's name." She also reversed her earlier interpretation about the serpent she saw in her first vision, now concluding it was a symbol of Satan.

We are not passing judgment upon Mrs. Dixon's honesty or sincerity, but we wonder why she didn't admit that her previous interpretation was wrong. It is obvious, however, that she did not receive the meaning of her visions from God. The Lord would not lead His servants to make mistakes of this nature and then later to issue a complete reversal. God's inspired prophets would not have made such errors.

A final, clinching reason for our refusal to consider any of today's seers as divinely inspired is our conviction that the gift of prophecy ceased when the Scriptures were completed. Prophets uttered truths they had received directly from God, and the Lord used this means of revelation during the years from the creation of man until the time of Malachi. From Malachi until John the Baptist came on the scene, Israel had no prophets. Then, in the brief period between Christ's ascension and the completion of the gospels and epistles, the gift of prophecy was present in the Church. But gradually the New Testament writings took the place of a prophetic ministry. The apostles were aware that God had given them special authority when they wrote, and that believers were to place greater value upon these gospels and epistles than so-called prophetic declarations. For example, although Paul was not speaking primarily of prophets, he definitely asserted the authoritative nature of his writings when he made the demand,

> . . . if any man obey not our word by this epistle, note that man, and have no company with him. . . (2 Thess. 3:14).

Again, writing to the Christians in Corinth, he said that his words were the very commandment of God, and that they constituted the standard by which God's people could evaluate the declarations of men considered to be prophets.

> If any man think himself to be a prophet, or spiritual, let him acknowledge that the things that I write unto you are the commandments of the Lord (1 Cor. 14:37).

The priority of these apostolic writings over the declarations of other men who claimed to be prophets is further indicated by the apostle John as he brought the book of Revelation to a close. He knew that he was writing the authoritative message of God, and therefore could issue this strong warning:

> For I testify unto every man that heareth the words of the prophecy of this book, If any man shall add unto these things, God shall add unto him the plagues that are written in this book;
> And if any man shall take away from the

words of the book of this prophecy, God shall take away his part from the tree of life, and out of the holy city, and from the things which are written in this book (Rev. 22:18, 19).

No one claiming a prophetic gift had any right to tamper with the written Word. It is obvious, therefore, that the inspired writing of the apostles gradually superseded prophetic utterances in the early church. Special gifts like prophecy, knowledge, wisdom, healings, and tongues were gradually withdrawn, and in 1 Corinthians 13 Paul declared that the quiet, unselfish pursuit of love is a far more excellent path than that of always desiring the more spectacular activities. He continued,

> . . . whether there be prophecies, they shall be done away; whether there be tongues, they shall cease; whether there be knowledge, it shall vanish away.
> For we know in part, and we prophecy in part.
> But when that which is perfect is come, then that which is in part shall be done away (1 Cor. 13:8-10).

The New Testament as a whole was not yet in existence when Paul wrote these words, but he declared that special gifts of the Holy Spirit such as prophecy and tongues would become a thing of the past. They would merge into the complete revelation of the New Testament and no longer be needed. They belonged to the childhood state of the Church; therefore, we conclude that the gift of prophecy cannot be in existence today. God has spoken in the Scriptures, and it is to them that we must turn to find His message to us. No one today can rightly claim that he speaks a message by direct inspiration of the Holy Spirit.

In summary, we do not believe that anyone today who claims to receive visions directly from the Lord should be acknowledged as a spiritual leader.

None of these so-called prophets are correct in every single prediction they make, and therefore they do not meet the test the Lord prescribed in Deuteronomy 18. Most of them are also guilty of disobeying the Biblical warnings of Paul against occultism. In addition, they tend to speak ambiguously and manifest an ignorance of what the Bible really teaches. Finally, we believe that we have logical, historical, and Biblical grounds for affirming that the gift of prophecy was temporary, and that it gave way and disappeared from the Church when the New Testament was completed.

II. ASTROLOGY

Of all the current methods of foretelling the future, the most popular is astrology. Astrologers claim that by observing the position of the sun, moon, fixed stars, and planets they can predict significant events that will take place on earth. Palm reading is another method of fortunetelling, but it is so closely related to astrology that it does not require special consideration. The person who engages in this practice divides the hand into seven mounds which are named after heavenly bodies — Venus, Mercury, Apollo (the sun), Saturn, Jupiter, Mars, and the Moon. In addition, the palm has four lines, which are "read" by the palmist. He calls them the heart, head, life, and fate lines, and sees each of them as having special significance. Everything we will say about the evils, dangers, and deceitfulness of astrology applies to palmistry as well.

In discussing astrology, one must first recognize that it is classified as a pseudoscience, and it should not be confused with astronomy, a legitimate field of study. Astrology originated about 5000 years ago in Mesopotamia and flourished in Assyria,

Babylonia, Egypt, Persia, and Greece. It began with people who worshiped the sun, moon, and the five known planets of that time as gods. They thought each of these seven deities owned a certain section of the heavens as his "house." They therefore established the zodiac, the wide belt of fixed stars that appear in the course of a year, and divided it into twelve "houses." As a result, there were twelve dwelling places for seven deities. The early astrologers decided that the sun and moon needed only one "house" each, and therefore assigned two dwelling places to Jupiter, Venus, Saturn, Mars, and Mercury. These planets had one "house" for the day and another for the night.

This heathen concept of the planets as gods with dwelling places in the heavens gradually developed into a detailed system of religion. Men carefully studied the heavenly bodies, and noted how the positions of the planets changed. They theorized that whenever two or more of these planets (which they considered gods) were positioned in a direct radial line or within a ten-degree angle, some extremely significant events would occur upon the earth. They called this a "conjunction" of the planets. Since the movement of the heavenly bodies is perfectly predictable, they could pinpoint the very hour such conjunctions would take place, and make favorable or unfavorable predictions based upon the meanings they had given to each of the "houses" through which the planet moved.

For many years educated men mingled their astrological superstitions with their studies of nature, mathematics, physics, and astronomy. Some have assumed that the Magi, who came to Jerusalem looking for the King of the Jews when Jesus was born, came because of an astrological sign. This is a mistaken assumption, and the idea should never be used as evidence that the New Testament condones the practice of astrology. Although the wise men as learned sages of the East undoubtedly shared in some of the superstitions of their day, the light that led them to make their journey to Jerusalem was a miraculously placed sign from God, not a mere configuration of the stars. It has been theorized that the conjunction of the planets Jupiter and Saturn, which took place in 747 A.U.C. (7 B.C.), or with Mars added in 748 A.U.C. (6 B.C.), led them to look for Jesus. This supposition is without validity, however. In the first place, the Bible nowhere declares that heavenly bodies in their normal movements furnish this kind of information. Second, a similar conjunction of planets had taken place about fifty-nine years earlier, but this had not led an investigating body to Jerusalem. Third, when planets move near to one another to form a conjunction, they are never so close that they appear as one star. Fourth, the light miraculously appeared over the house where Jesus was living when the Magi arrived. These factors prove conclusively that the light in the heavens was a miracle. We repeat, the wise men who presented their gifts to Jesus did not receive information of His birth through astrology.

A popular outgrowth of astrology is the horoscope, a chart of the zodiacal signs and the position of the planets by which astrologers attempt to predict future events. The vast majority of the newspapers in the United States carry them daily, and the preparation of these horoscopes occupies about 10,000 full-time and 175,000 part-time workers in our country alone. These columns make predictions and give advice on the basis of the sign of the zodiac under which a person was born, and how it relates to the position of the planet on the date the horoscope appears in the newspaper.

Astrologers have given names to the twelve constellations which were originally termed "the houses for the gods." They believe these constellations have definite characteristics which distinguish them from one another, and which largely predetermine the personality of each individual. For example, if one came into the world between December 22 and January 19, he was born under the sign named Capricorn, which is the Goat. His personality would therefore bear some of the characteristics the goat is supposed to symbolize. Birth between January 20 and February 18 places one under the sign of Aquarius, which is the Water Bearer; between February 19 and March 20, Pisces, which is the Fish; between March 21 and April 19, Aries, which is the Ram; between April 20 and May 20, Taurus, which is the Bull; between May 21 and June 21, Gemini, which is The Twins; between June 22 and July 22, Cancer, which is the Crab; between July 23 and August 22, Leo, which is the Lion; between August 23 and September 22, Virgo, which is the Virgin; between September 23 and October 23, Libra, which is the Scales; between October 24 and November 21, Scorpio, which is the Scorpion; and between November 22 and December 21, Sagittarius, which is the Archer. One can see that this is a highly subjective field, and that it gives free rein to the imagination. How tragic that thousands of people faithfully read the horoscopes printed in newspapers and magazines, sincerely believing the predictions they make and the advice they give are valid. The blindness of people who reject God is almost beyond comprehension.

In addition, individuals willing to pay the fee may also purchase a personal horoscope. In fact, computers are able to turn out a 10,000-word personal horoscope reading in two minutes. The precise moment of a person's birth is recorded, and then the exact position of the heavenly bodies at that time is ascertained. This becomes the starting point for the computer to begin its program. The practitioners who sell horoscopes provide a great deal of incentive for the purchase of their services by saying that some of the information given is not an absolute, unchangeable decree. Some of the prognostications are in the form of conditional declarations which will depend to a great extent upon the circumstances. For example, a person is encouraged to read horoscopes to be forewarned about personality difficulties and impending disasters so he can take steps to avoid the problems and dangers. This makes the purchase of personal horoscopes extremely inviting.

Though astrology is popular today, it must be condemned as unscriptural, unreliable, devious, and dangerous. Christians should not only avoid it, but also be informed so they can warn others.

As previously noted, the Bible strongly forbids all forms of occultism, including astrology.

> There shall not be found among you anyone who maketh his son or his daughter pass through the fire, or who useth divination, or an *observer of times,* or an enchanter, or a witch,
>
> Or a charmer, or a consultor of mediums, or a wizard, or a necromancer.
>
> For all that do these things are an abomination unto the LORD; and because of these abominations the LORD thy God doth drive them out from before thee (Deut. 18:10-12).

Moses gave as one of the reasons the danger that it would lead the people into heathenism. Astrology originated with pagans who considered the stars to be gods, and anyone who began to dabble in this pseudoscientific practice would inevitably be drawn into the superstition and false beliefs inherent to the system. Therefore God pronounced death by stoning for any Israelite who participated in star worship.

> If there be found among you, within any of thy gates which the LORD thy God giveth thee, man or woman who hath wrought wickedness in the sight of the LORD thy God, in transgressing his covenant,
>
> And hath gone and served other gods, and worshiped them, either the sun, or moon, or any of the hosts of heaven, which I have not commanded,
>
> And it be told thee, and thou hast heard of it, and inquired diligently, and, behold, it is true, and the thing certain, that such abomination is wrought in Israel;
>
> Then shalt thou bring forth that man or that woman, who hath committed that wicked thing, unto thy gates, even that man or that woman, and shalt stone them with stones, till they die (Deut. 17:2-5).

Later in Israel's history, the prophet Isaiah proclaimed judgment upon the nation, and in biting sarcasm dared the people to seek deliverance through the sorcerers and the Babylonian astrologers in whom they had placed their confidence. His words stand as a sharp denunciation of astrology, and indicate that God considered it a false religion.

> Stand now with thine enchantments, and with the multitude of thy sorceries, in which thou hast labored from thy youth, if so be thou shalt be able to profit, if so be thou mayest prevail.
>
> Thou art wearied in the multitude of thy counsels. Let now the astrologers, the stargazers, the monthly prognosticators, stand up, and save thee from these things that shall come upon thee (Isa. 47:12, 13).

The prophet Jeremiah also warned the people of God that they were not to believe that omens for evil could be read in the heavens. He declared,

> Thus saith the LORD, Learn not the way of the nations, and be not dismayed at the signs of heaven; for the nations are dismayed at them (Jer. 10:2).

Since astrology had its origin in the idolatrous practices of heathenism, and could not be disassociated from superstition and false beliefs, God has forbidden His children to become involved in it.

A second reason for the absolute prohibition of astrology in the Old Testament is that it is an attempt to ascertain the will of God by other means than those which He has appointed. The believer who disobeys the admonitions of Scripture will be chastened by the Lord and may be opening the door for demonic attacks upon his personality.

Horoscopes also are unreliable, and the person who spends time and money on them may allow himself to be victimized by fraudulent people. Remember, astrology is not a science or legitimate field of scholastic endeavor. Instead, it is the means by which some people attain fabulous wealth without really helping anyone else. Horoscopes are not a reliable or valuable source of information about anything. The people who are writing horoscopes and promoting astrology are cashing in on the gullibility and ignorance of the public. Newspapers and magazines pay a fat fee for their astrological columns, and many editors and publishers undoubtedly do so reluctantly, realizing that the horoscopes have very little value. But they are compelled to purchase these columns in order to maintain a high subscription level. Dr. Kurt Koch cites a telling instance which reveals the nonsensical nature of the daily readings for which such a high price is paid.

> The editor of a large daily reported that on a certain day the delivery of astromantic material from his supplier came too late. In order not to annoy his subscribers, he simply went to his old files and inserted in the column one of the older, forgotten weekly horoscopes. Not one of the 100,000 readers noticed the "deception." So he concluded further, if this goes so well, then why should I not spare myself the weekly cost for the material? So for three months he filled the column with old horoscopic material. At last a reader wrote in, remarking that the sign of the zodiac could not check with the month. At last his ruse was perceived and now for the sake of caution he had to contact his supplier again to get "trustworthy" horoscopy! (Koch, *Christian Counseling and Occultism,* p. 79).

Joseph Bayly also points out that astrologers often make errors that are conveniently forgotten by their faithful followers. An example of such a "monumental goof" was their prediction of a California earthquake of April, 1969.

> Astrologers warned that a large slice of California — some of them said the whole state — would fall into the Pacific Ocean as a result of a devastating earthquake. People moved away because of their faith in the prediction, and Governor Ronald Reagan had to issue a statement that he'd been planning for some time to take his vacation outside the State during April. What happened during April? Nothing.
>
> On October, 20, 1968, Jeane Dixon's syndicated column had to be hastily withdrawn from newspapers in which it would have appeared. Reason: Mrs. Dixon had written, "I still stand on my New Year's prediction and see no marriage for Jackie in the near future." That turned out to be the day of Jacqueline Kennedy's wedding to Aristotle Onassis.

British astrologer Maurice Woodruff claims 75 percent accuracy for his predictions. Like Jeane Dixon and Carroll Righter, he makes a lot of money. But it's being paid to foretell the future of others, not by making investments in the light of the future for himself. Among his failures are the birth of a male child to Frank and Mia Sinatra — a year before they were divorced without any children; an overnight end to the Vietnam war in April, 1969 (Mrs. Dixon had already predicted peace in 1965); and the marriage of Lynda Bird Johnson to actor George Hamilton. (Bayly, *What About Horoscopes?* pp. 18, 19. David C. Cook Publishing Company.)

I certainly would not be willing to make important decisions on the basis of the prognostications and advice of astrologers. Almost any intelligent person, without claiming a psychic gift or magical source of information, could make a series of predictions and be quite sure of being right seventy-five percent of the time. He need only be careful to make most of his predictions of such a nature that the chance of their coming to pass would be far better than the odds against it.

In addition to being unscriptural and unreliable, horoscopes are often devious in nature. By this I mean that their predictions and advice are often written so that they can be interpreted a number of ways. In fact, they seldom say anything very specific. Joseph Bayly calls attention to this by referring to the horoscopes that appeared in certain newspapers in Chicago on 1 December 1969, entering the homes of thousands of people just a few hours before the first draft lottery was held. One would have expected that these columns by the astrologers would have spared the young men of the United States and their families the needless anxiety of waiting until the draft lottery had actually been held before knowing how they stood in the draft. But did anyone find out what number he would receive through horoscopes? Not on your life! It turned out that the young men who were born on September 14 drew number 1, and this meant that they would be drafted almost immediately or as soon as their deferment ended. To the people born on September 14 Jeane Dixon's advice was: "You are close to your best today in material affairs if you will listen to the urging of your intuitive powers." From Carroll Righter came the enlightening words, "Make plans for self-improvement in the near future."

A similar kind of double-talk was addressed to the young men born on June 7, the fellows who were given the highest number in that first draft lottery. Most of them could be assured that they would never be called into the service. Did the astrologers foresee the good news that awaited these young men the next morning? Apparently not! Jeane Dixon told them, "Tonight hold a simple gathering of friends with different viewpoints." Carroll Righter's advice was, "Take it easy in the evening." It is obvious that the writers of these columns had absolutely no idea of the outcome of the draft lottery that would be held the night of December 1, and that they tried to produce a sentence which would cover almost any situation or eventuality.

Horoscopes also are dangerous. The person who consults them for information about his future is subject not only to the ordinary perils that stem from disobedience to God, divine chastening, and possibly demonic attacks, but also to the power of suggestion. For example, if one is warned that during a designated period of time he will be vulnerable to certain dangers, he may unconsciously fulfill the prediction and actually bring disaster into his life. On the other hand, a person who is told that he will be lucky on a given day may do something reckless and bring harm to himself or others. The Lord has good reason for withholding from us detailed information of tomorrow's joys and sorrows. It is far better for us to live without this knowledge. If a couple knew that the husband and father would die at a young age, leaving his wife and small children, they would not be able to enjoy the present nearly as much as they can without such precognition. God has promised to provide grace for His children when the difficulties and trials actually come. And He does!

Remember, the Bible forbids all forms of fortunetelling. Therefore every Christian must avoid it, gladly leaving the future with the Lord and using the present to walk in obedience to that which He has declared in His Word. Men should never turn to the occult in an effort to break through the limitations of knowledge God has established. Moses gave this counsel when he said,

> The secret things belong unto the LORD our God; but those things which are revealed belong unto us and to our children forever, that we may do all the words of this law (Deut. 29:29).

We who know Christ do not need the prognostications of Jeane Dixon or any other so-called prophet. It is not necessary for us to consult horoscopes or have someone tell us our future by reading our palm. Our Christian faith has given us something far better. We have been brought into union with the triune God. The Father loved us from all eternity, and still does; the Son came into this world as a human being to provide for our salvation and now abides in Heaven as our forerunner and intercessor; the Holy Spirit lives within our hearts. This triune God will indeed meet our every need.

The future? We can leave it with Him. We have confidence that our sins have been forgiven because Jesus paid the price on the cross of Calvary. We are assured that death cannot harm us, because Jesus Christ destroyed both its sting and its power when He rose from the grave. In fact, we may never experience death, for our Savior may come at any moment to translate us into His presence. In either case, we need not fear. If we are called upon to die, death will come to us not as a hideous monster but as a bright messenger from the other shore. The angels of God will only close our eyes and kiss away our breath, and hand in hand with Jesus Christ we will step from time into eternity. Even the body, the imperfect house in which our spirit now lives, is precious in God's sight, for each of us will receive it again some day in resurrection glory.

When one is assured that his sin has been forgiven and that death's power has been destroyed, he can face both the present and the future with optimism and courage. Let us obey our Savior's exhortation:

> Therefore, I say unto you, Be not anxious for your life, what ye shall eat, or what ye shall drink; nor yet for your body, what ye shall put on. Is not the life more than food and the body more than raiment?
>
> Behold the fowls of the air; for they sow not, neither do they reap, nor gather into barns, yet your heavenly Father feedeth them. Are ye not much better than they?
>
> Which of you by being anxious can add one cubit unto his stature?
>
> And why are ye anxious for raiment? Consider the lilies of the field, how they grow; they toil not, neither do they spin,
>
> And yet I say unto you that even Solomon, in all his glory, was not arrayed like one of these.

Wherefore, if God so clothe the grass of the field, which today is, and tomorrow is cast into the oven, shall he not much more clothe you, O ye of little faith?

Therefore, be not anxious saying, What shall we eat? or, What shall we drink? or, With what shall we be clothed?

For after all these things do the Gentiles seek. For your heavenly Father knoweth that ye have need of all these things.

But seek ye first the kingdom of God, and his righteousness, and all these things shall be added unto you.

Be, therefore, not anxious about tomorrow; for tomorrow will be anxious for the things of itself. Sufficient unto the day is its own evil (Matt. 6:25-34).

We have a heavenly Father who has proven His love for us by sending Christ to be our Savior. He has shown us that He places high value upon us. If He is concerned enough about the birds to feed them, and about lilies to make them exquisite in their beauty, will He not also meet every need of His children both for time and for eternity? Instead of worrying about the future and trying to gather information about it, trust the Lord to meet your needs day by day. The old hymn which tells us to "trust and obey" sums up the Christian life very well. The believer who walks this pathway will find joy, peace, and deep satisfaction. The whole realm of occultism offers him nothing he does not already truly enjoy.

6

Satan and Witchcraft

Satan and witchcraft are very much in vogue today. Right now an old house painted black stands on California Street in San Francisco, and it is called the "church of Satan." Its leader, Anton Szandor La Vey, calls himself the "high priest of Satan," and declares that he has dedicated his organization to the proclamation of complete sexual permissiveness, unbridled vengeance, and unrestrained greed. He calls the fireplace mantel of the house his "living altar," and a nude priestess is in full display before the "worshipers" when he holds his services. In Toledo, Ohio, Herbert Arthur Sloan heads a similar "church" dedicated to Satan. The fad seems to be catching on, and it may be only a matter of time before every large city has a similar center of devil worship.

Witches and witchcraft also are on the increase. Movies and television programs often present beautiful young women as witches, usually portraying them as lovable and mischievous, not evil and cruel. Samantha of the television series *Bewitched* is a far cry from the familiar picture of the old hag who rides a broomstick. One of the children's Saturday cartoons, a program called *Sabrina*, is about a teenage witch. Both are presented as harmless and amusing caricatures of the traditional sorceress.

A study of the increasing number who call themselves witches reveals some startling information. Sybil Leek, who lives in Melbourne Beach, Florida, calls herself "the most famous witch in the world," and flies (by jet, that is) to every major city in the United States to promote her craft. She claims 400 "authentic witches" as her personal friends, and declares that about eight million people in the world today are witches. She believes that increasing numbers will turn to witchcraft, for people are "searching for a religion where they don't have to live a God-like life, a religion that acknowledges them as human beings." Apparently she thinks that the moral demands of the Christian faith are in violation of our basic humanity.

As we address ourselves to a discussion of this amazing resurgence of witchcraft in our sophisticated, scientific world, let us first take the time to define our subject. Then we will examine the various kinds of magic allegedly performed by those we categorize as witches.

I. THE NATURE OF WITCHCRAFT

One must recognize that over the course of centuries the ideas about witches and their activity have changed. The medieval notion of witchcraft is far different from that of the Bible, and today's self-styled witches usually resemble the ancient concept more than that of the Middle Ages.

The Old Testament word which denotes a witch is *kashaph*. It is used in various forms, and most often is translated "sorcerer," "sorcery," or "sorceries." This means that a witch was a person who used magical formulas, incantations, or mutterings to exercise control over the unseen world. Other kinds of occultism, though equally condemned, were not regarded in the Old Testament as witchcraft. The individual who sought to communicate with the dead was called a necromancer, and this practice was not synonymous with sorcery. Similarly, foretelling the future by means of "reading" the livers of animals, the signs in the heavens, the flight of birds, or the movements of particles in a liquid, though also forbidden, were not considered equivalent to witchcraft. Strictly speaking, the term "sorcerer" or "witch" referred to any person who summoned invisible powers to help in casting spells or performing feats of magic. Moses forbade the entire range of occultic activity for the Israelites, and carefully distinguished between its various forms when he declared:

> There shall not be found among you anyone who maketh his son or his daughter pass through the fire, or who useth divination, or an observer of times, or an enchanter, or a witch,
> Or a charmer, or a consultor of mediums, or a wizard, or a necromancer.
> For all that do these things are an abomination unto the LORD; and because of these abominations the LORD thy God doth drive them out from before thee (Deut. 18:10-12).

It isn't easy for us to accurately define and completely separate the specific practices Moses names. In general, it may be said that the enchanter (worker of magic), the witch (incantation-using sorcerer), the charmer (snake-handling hypnotist), and the wizard (the psychically gifted person who appeared to possess extra-sensory perception) came under the general Old Testament heading of witchcraft.

In medieval times the concept of sorcery was different from that of the Old Testament. A witch was considered to be a person who had sold her soul to Satan in exchange for magical powers. She was said to engage in sexual relations with demons, and people thought she cast evil spells upon animals and people. These witches were always looked upon as dangerous and malevolent, while those of Biblical times, though practicing a craft forbidden by God, often were regarded by the heathen as benefactors of society. The medieval idea that some women actually sold themselves to the devil led to events which are a dark blot in church history. The combination of superstition, cruelty, and mass hysteria brought about the persecution and execution of many women on charges of witchcraft. Some historians estimate that in Europe alone more than nine million suspected witches were put to death upon the flimsiest of evidence. Today we realize that the vast majority of these unfortunates never made a pact with the devil, did not possess magical powers, and did not harm anyone. Most of them were ignorant women who came under suspicion because their words and actions departed from what was considered the norm. Some no doubt were brain-damaged, while others suffered from neuroses or psychotic conditions.

The concept of witchcraft today differs in some details from both that of Biblical and medieval times. In contrast to the sorcerers of antiquity who believed in many gods, a large percentage of today's witches are not deeply religious and do not consider their powers to be attributable to the supernatural. Most of these self-proclaimed witches do not speak of making a covenant with Satan, although this dedication to the devil is basic to black magic, as we shall see later. Contemporary witches do insist, however, that they are able to contact and utilize powers that come from the unseen world.

Witchcraft today emulates that of the pre-Christian era in many respects. Its practitioners often organize into covens, a group of six male and six female witches with a high priest or priestess. They meet monthly at the time of the full moon, and at eight other festivals called sabbats throughout the year. *The New York Times* describes the Halloween sabbat at the home of Raymond Buckland, a Britisher with a Ph.D. in anthropology.

First the witches remove their clothes and bathe in salt water to purify themselves. Then, still nude (sky-clad, as they call it) they descend to the basement and step inside a 9-foot circle that is drawn about them with a 400-year-old sword by Mrs. Buckland, the high priestess, who is known in the craft as Lady Rowen. A bewitching ambience is provided by music from a tape recorder and incense burned in a brass censor.

Once inside the circle, the witches sing, chant, dance with broomsticks in commemoration of an ancient fertility rite, drink tea and wine, and listen to the high priestess read from the Book of Shadows.

The ceremony ends after Lady Rowen, dressed in only a silver crown, bracelet, necklace, and green leather garter belt, takes a horned helmet and places it on the head of her husband, the high priest, who is known as Robat. This signifies that power has been transferred from the high priestess who reigns during the six months of summer, to the high priest, who rules during the six winter months.

It is obvious that this is a return to ancient pagan practices, and that witchcraft is indeed a false religious system. It even has its own Bible, called *The Book of Shadows,* a compilation of rituals and chants drawn from various books of magic by which the practitioners produce their spells and charms. Witchcraft is therefore a religion that denies or distorts the holy Scriptures, ignores or perverts the doctrine of Christ, and offers no deliverance from the guilt and power of sin.

II. THE PRACTICE OF MAGIC

In popular thinking, the term "magic" refers to the tricks of a sleight-of-hand artist, the optical illusions created by a clever trickster, or the cunning exhibition of seemingly supernatural powers by money-hungry charlatans. Undoubtedly many of the amazing demonstrations performed by such people have a completely naturalistic explanation, but honest scholars who have investigated occultic phenomena in many parts of the world agree that science at present is unable to account for some of the apparently supernatural events they have witnessed. The Bible also sets forth the view that not all magic is merely hocus-pocus.

A. The Biblical portrayal of magic. The Scriptures acknowledge that real superhuman power can be accomplished through sorcery, but clearly teach that the source of such manifestations is evil.

The Egyptian magicians actually were able to change their rods into serpents by throwing them on the ground. Some say these rods were really snakes which had been hypnotized into becoming as rigid as a cane, but even so we must admit that no scientist today can explain how these men were able to perform this feat. They also were successful in changing water into blood, and in producing a miraculous multiplication of frogs, thus apparently duplicating what Moses and Aaron had done by God's supernatural power. (See Exod. 7 and 8.)

The Egyptian sorcerers undoubtedly believed their gods gave them the ability to perform these amazing exploits, and they viewed their encounter with Moses and Aaron as a contest to determine whether or not their gods were more powerful than Jehovah. The Bible implies that supernatural beings take advantage of the practices of heathenism to further enslave their adherents, but declares that these invisible agents are neither holy angels nor gods. It states that they are demons — spirit beings who rebelled against God and now are dedicated to opposing Him. For this reason, Moses and Aaron convincingly demonstrated the superiority of Jehovah over these demonic forces. When Aaron's rod became a serpent, it swallowed up those the Egyptians had cast to the ground. The greater power of God also was manifested when the pagan sorcerers were unable to remove the plague of frogs, but Moses simply prayed to the Lord, and "the frogs died out of the houses, out of the villages, and out of the fields" (Exod. 8:13). God's servants then brought about the third plague, a changing of dust into lice, a judgment which made life almost unbearable for man and beast. This time the magicians of Egypt were unable to duplicate the miracle, nor could they bring about the sudden death of the pests. They therefore humbly acknowledged, "This is the finger of God" (Exod. 8:19). In this manner, the Lord demonstrated His absolute superiority over the powers of evil which the Egyptians worshiped as gods. It is important for us to note again that the Bible does not indicate that the magicians were mere frauds.

A careful study of the history of Egypt, Babylon, and other nations of antiquity reveals that heathen priests accomplished many unusual feats, and kept the people under subjection through what appeared to be supernatural abilities. In seeking to understand some of the mysterious phenomena of heathenism, we must bear in mind the declaration of the apostle Paul, "But I say that the things which the Gentiles sacrifice, they sacrifice to demons" (1 Cor. 10:20). The apostle was definitely saying that the worship of idols involved more than merely bowing down to lifeless images. Furthermore, the fact that the Bible repeatedly forbids sorcery, divination, and every other form of occultism is evidence that God links these practices with actual demonic power. We repeat, the death penalty would not have been the prescribed punishment for all mediums, fortunetellers, and sorcerers if they were only quacks guilty of deception for gain.

Critics of the Bible insist that its attitude toward some forms of witchcraft is inconsistent, and even sincere believers have been puzzled by several passages which appear to condone these practices. A careful examination of these instances, however, reveals that such critical assertions are unwarranted.

Genesis 30:14-18 records the story of Leah and Rachel bargaining for mandrakes, showing that they believed these so-called "love apples" increased a woman's fertility. But the fact that Jacob's wives held to this ancient concept does not necessarily indicate that the Bible expresses approval. Then, too, modern investigation has shown that some primitive medicines, scorned by medics a generation or two ago, actually do possess qualities which make them valuable. At any rate, this passage of Scripture does not indicate that the Bible encourages the use of magic.

In another instance of apparent superstition, Jacob peeled the bark from saplings to give them a spotted appearance because he believed that the offspring of the cattle bred before them would then be speckled and spotted. This story is declared to be an indication that the writer of Genesis held to the notion that the color of the unborn young would be affected by what the female animal saw at the time of impregnation. (See Gen. 30:37-43.) A careful study of the entire account reveals, however, the truth that God actually was controlling the breeding process through the laws of heredity, not by means of Jacob's efforts. The angel of the

Lord later told the patriarch that the male animals possessed genetic characteristics which brought about the birth of so many striped, speckled, and spotted animals. (See Gen. 31:11, 12.) Therefore, we can assert with confidence that this passage of Scripture in no way encourages the use of magic.

The statement of Joseph to his brothers about his silver cup also poses a problem for Bible students, because his words seem to indicate that he used it for purposes of divination. After the steward had hidden the cup in Benjamin's sack of grain, Joseph told him what he was to do and say. The King James Version records Joseph's instructions as follows, "Up, follow after the men; and when thou dost overtake them, say unto them, Wherefore have ye rewarded evil for good? Is not this it in which my Lord drinketh, and whereby indeed he divineth? Ye have done evil in so doing" (Gen. 44:4, 5). Scholars today know that the heathen sorcerers of Joseph's day often sprinkled small particles of gold or silver into a cup of water, or poured a small amount of oil in it, and then "read" the resulting design in the cup for omens. While it is possible that Joseph fell into this sinful and heathenish practice, we doubt very much that he did, for he had one of the finest characters of all the men portrayed in the entire Old Testament. In addition, we can present good reason for our conviction that Joseph never really used the cup to find out about the unknown.

In the first place, Joseph did not need such sources of information. God had spoken to him through dreams and other forms of revelation, and therefore Joseph did possess knowledge ordinarily hidden to men. In that sense he *was* able to "divine." His instructions to his steward may be translated, "Is it not from this cup that my Lord drinks, and *concerning which* he will assuredly divine?" In other words, Joseph made it clear that he possessed a power which would enable him to find out what had happened to the cup. (We must remember that Joseph was play-acting in order to test his brothers. He wanted them to be puzzled by the knowledge he possessed, and did not want to disclose his real identity at this time. For this reason, he did not speak of obtaining information directly from God.) This interpretation of verse 5 fits well with the statement of Joseph recorded in verse 15, "What deed is this that ye have done? Know ye not that such a man as I can certainly divine?" He let his brothers know that he was a special person with unusual powers of perception, but did not reveal the source of his ability. Later he told them about his faith in God. Therefore, the story of Joseph and the silver cup is certainly not an indication of Biblical approval of magic, and the likelihood exists that Joseph never practiced the heathen customs of his day.

Certain elements of the Mosaic law sometimes are thought to be a form of magic. In Numbers 5, for example, we are told that if a man suspected his wife of unfaithfulness, he was to take her to the priest for trial. The woman would then drink a liquid potion to determine her guilt or innocence. If certain physical results became apparent immediately, she was deemed guilty. If not, she was innocent. On the surface this appears to be a superstitious practice, but when we remember that Israel lived under a theocracy and that God had ordained this test, we can believe He would in this manner declare infallibly the guilt or innocence of the person being tried.

The Urim and Thummim as a means of revelation and the long hair of Samson as the secret of his strength are further examples of divinely ordered and controlled phenomena which cannot be compared to the magic of the heathen. Therefore, we can say assuredly that nothing in the Old Testament or the New can be properly interpreted as divine sanction of sorcery or magic.

Shortly before the Exile, the prophet Ezekiel delivered a scorching denunciation of women who were using amulets and veils in a magic ritual to bring joy or sadness, blessing or cursing, even life or death to certain individuals.

Likewise, thou son of man, set thy face against the daughters of thy people, who prophesy out of their own heart, and prophesy thou against them,

And say, Thus saith the Lord GOD: Woe to the women that sew amulets upon all wrists, and make kerchiefs for the head of every person of stature to hunt souls! Will ye hunt the souls of my people, and will ye save the souls alive that come unto you?

And will ye pollute me among my people for handfuls of barley and for pieces of bread, to slay the souls that should not die, and to save the souls alive that should not live, by your lying to my people that hear your lies?

Wherefore, thus saith the Lord GOD: Behold, I am against your amulets, with which ye there hunt the souls to make them fly; and I will tear them from your arms, and will let the souls go, even the souls that ye hunt to make them fly.

Your kerchiefs also will I tear, and deliver my people out of your hand, and they shall be no more in your hand to be hunted; and ye shall know that I am the LORD.

Because with lies ye have made the heart of the righteous sad, whom I have not made sad; and strengthened the hands of the wicked, that he should not return from his wicked way, by promising him life;

Therefore, ye shall see no more vanity, nor

divine divinations; for I will deliver my people out of your hand; and ye shall know that I am the LORD (Ezek. 13:17-23).

Exactly what these women did is not easy to ascertain. Some Bible students have conjectured that they performed a rite in which they symbolically bound up the soul of a person so that the individual would gradually waste away and die. Then, for a fee they would bring about his release. Other scholars think that Ezekiel describes features of "sympathetic magic," whereby the sorceress fastened something around her own wrists or enshrouded her own head to place a curse upon a specific individual. In either case, the practice of these women appeared to have consequences so serious as to warrant divine condemnation and a prophetic declaration that God would deliver His people from their grasp.

In summary, the Old Testament acknowledges the existence of real magic, and consistently condemns it in every form. Furthermore, the rites and ceremonies prescribed for Israel were not equivalent to the practices of the heathen, but were instructions that came directly from God and over which He would exercise control.

B. Black and white magic. Contemporary forms of magic are being studied carefully by parapsychologists. (Parapsychology is the study of apparently supernatural phenomena such as telepathy, clairvoyance, apparitions, and related forms of ESP.) Researchers in this field who operate from a completely naturalistic standpoint deny the existence of a personal devil or evil spirits. They may speak of two vital forces in the universe, however, one working upward in an evolutionary manner, and the other counteracting these ascending steps. These investigators of psychic phenomena do not make any effort to explain the origin of these invisible powers, and simply declare that some people have special psychic gifts which give them access to these forces. They may even say that some religious practitioners appear to have superhuman power, and refer to their work as white magic. They may also acknowledge that some individuals can mysteriously bring harm to their enemies, and this evil use of power they call black magic. The majority of these parapsychologists insist, however, that they do not believe in a personal God or the devil, and simply affirm that at the present time we do not fully understand some of the esoteric powers in this universe.

The Christian student of occultic activity has a distinct advantage over the naturalist, for he accepts the reality of a personal God and an invisible world of angels and evil spirits. This does not mean that he rejects a scientific approach to the problems that are encountered. He must avoid the temptation to declare dogmatically that every unexplainable occurrence is the result of supernatural activity — either by God or the forces of evil. Some manifestations that now puzzle us may in the future be understood within the framework of the natural. The fact remains, however, that Satan is a real personality, and that a multitude of evil spirits have joined him in opposition to God and His people. The Bible records numerous instances which clearly reveal their activity, and we have good reason to believe that some of the unexplainable phenomena in evidence today are the works of these demonic beings.

Practitioners of black magic usually declare openly that they are serving the devil. Many of them say they have made a pact with Satan, and some have indicated their allegiance to him by signing a document with their own blood. Missionaries have reported that pacts with the devil are not at all unknown among many primitive peoples. Reputable followers of Christ are convinced that these religious leaders actually can bring illness or death to people through ritualistic incantations. Black magic is practiced extensively today in parts of Germany, France, and Switzerland, as well as in primitive cultures. Dr. Kurt Koch cites numerous instances of conjurers casting spells which have brought about the death of animals and even humans. He also tells of amazing healings, but points out that when a person is cured of a physical disease by such a practitioner, he usually suffers such severe mental depression that the new condition is worse than the old. As one reads the examples of black magic — cattle being milked dry in a mysterious manner, the sudden unexplainable death of animals, healings followed by terrible psychic disturbances, and the appearance of frightful apparitions — he finds his credulity stretched almost to the breaking point. If one has not witnessed such occurrences, he is likely to dismiss these reports as untrustworthy. But serious scholars who have investigated these accounts do not deny the reality of such phenomena. They may not believe them to be the work of Satan or evil spirits, but they admit that many of them cannot be explained at the present time. Professor Adolph Koberle, from the University of Tubingen, in the introduction to *Christian Counseling and Occultism,* says:

> Readers who approach this study with a purely rationalistic bent will experience spiritual difficulty in following the author in many areas because we have here a report of cases and experiences which seems to conflict with all sound

human intelligence. But perhaps such persons can by this book be brought to listen, since the author himself first tries the immanent solution of the problems and only where this is proved to fail does he break out and propose the added dimension, the dimension of the eternal. Even though this book may evoke contradictions here and there — from medics and pastors, from parapsychologists and psychotherapists — yet the questions that are here posed cannot be evaded by any person who concerns himself in a genuine and responsible manner with a fruitful diagnosis and a helpful therapy (Dr. Kurt Koch, *Christian Counseling and Occultism*, 1965, p. 6).

This quotation indicates that sane, scholarly, and sincere men have examined the apparently superhuman powers evidenced in black magic and other forms of occultism, and made every effort to find naturalistic explanations, before finally concluding that Satan and evil spirits are actually at work.

Black magic as a specific form of witchcraft has its own literature. *The Sixth and Seventh Books of Moses* are the primary source, and are well known in Europe. They constitute one volume, and are alleged to have been written by Moses himself. Strangely enough, they maintain that this great national leader was a servant of Satan, and set forth detailed instructions for establishing a mystical relationship with the devil. This book tells its readers how they can gain power through black magic over all the people they will encounter both in this world and the next. It makes this solemn assertion: "To whatever person possesses this book at any given time, Lucifer makes promise to carry out his commands, but only as long as he possesses this book." Dr. Koch comments on the strange and sinister nature of this writing by saying, "In the many cases which the pastor-counselors have come to know, there is no possessor of *The Sixth and Seventh Books of Moses* who have no psychic complication" (*Christian Counseling and Occultism*, p. 134).

A number of other books on magic which are commonly circulated are: *The Spiritual Shield; The Spring Book; The Eighth to Thirteenth Books of Moses; The Little Book of Romanus; The Genuine Fiery Dragon; The Black Raven; Saints' Blessing;* and *Enchanted Words of the Black Forest.* Not all of these works belong specifically to the art of black magic, but those who practice it use them to a greater or lesser degree.

White magic is declared by its practitioners to be in direct opposition to black magic. Whereas black magic includes an open allegiance with the powers of darkness, in white magic the name of God is invoked, and Biblical phrases are utilized. Most people who practice it, however, have no understanding of the basic doctrines of the Christian faith. Some possibly are endowed with an unexplainable psychic power, and their desire to use it was not totally selfish at the beginning. But many find very soon that they become enslaved to a yearning for self-exaltation. The Radio Bible Class has received letters from a number of people who for a time had engaged in a "healing ministry" of this kind, but who abandoned it because it led to a gradual departure from God. Although some cult leaders and those classified as healers are no doubt psychically endowed people, they are using the name of God and Christ in a manner that violates the Lord's will.

The danger of mistaking an enigmatic psychic power for the gift of the Lord must be recognized. Dr. Kurt Koch points out that Dr. Henry Drummond, fellow-worker of D. L. Moody, possessed psychic ability which enabled him to have mental power over persons who were miles away. While working with Moody, Drummond found that he could hypnotically influence the large crowds who had gathered, but concluded that to use this power would be a hindrance to the activity of the Holy Spirit. He prayed that the Lord would take this psychic gift away from him, and his prayer was answered. Had Dr. Drummond decided to exercise this ability, he would soon have established a worldwide reputation as a great healer. But his accomplishments would not have honored the Lord, and real blessings would not have resulted from his ministry. (See Dr. Kurt Koch, *Occult Bondage and Deliverance*, pp. 42-57.)

Dr. Merrill F. Unger sums up the distinction between religious white magic and Biblical faith and prayer as follows:

> In Biblical faith, trust is placed solely in the Lord Jesus. In white magic it is deflected to someone else (the human agent) or to something else (one's own faith, etc.). In the Biblical prayer of faith, the praying person subjects himself to the will of God. In white magic the help of God is demanded under the assumption that exercising such power is in accordance with God's will. In white magic the Christian markings are mere decorations that camouflage the magical means for knowledge or power (Merrill F. Unger, *Demons in the World Today*, p. 86).

C. Neutral magic. Some authorities in the field of parapsychology speak of "natural" or "neutral" magic. They use this term to describe phenomena which cannot be fully explained scientifically, but which take place without reference to either God or the devil.

In the realm of the physical are the inexplicable feats usually associated with spiritists. Objects of furniture and people sometimes mysteriously leave the ground and appear to float through the air. These occurrences are called "levitations." In close relationship to levitations is "telekinesis," a phenomenon which takes place when a psychically gifted person apparently moves objects by concentrating on them. A few years ago most scientifically minded people were convinced that such demonstrations were accomplished by the use of clever mechanical devices, but in many instances intensive scientific tests and checks have not uncovered any evidence of trickery. As a result, students in this field simply affirm that no one knows how these things take place. Another phenomenon closely allied to levitations and telekinesis is called "apport." Solid objects which disappear from a room are found an instant later in a location hundreds of miles away. Parapsychologists conjecture that the physical matter dissolves into pure energy and thus is able to pass through closed walls.

No serious student who has investigated these occurrences denies that they actually take place, but a great deal of research and careful study must be done to gain a full understanding of levitations, telekinesis, and apports. Ever since Einstein, no true scientist can say that such phenomena are an impossibility. While it could be that natural forces will be found to account for some of these amazing occurrences, it also is likely that evil spirits play a part in many instances.

Another enigma in the realm of the physical is the fact that in Europe some people diagnose and treat severe physical diseases through the magical use of a rod and pendulum. The pendulum is set in motion over the patient's body to find the cause of the illness, and then magic is used to bring about healing. No doubt the people who use this method often fail to help the patient, and undoubtedly a large percentage of the healings are only psycho-somatic. Investigators generally agree, however, that in some instances the rod and pendulum method appears to bring amazing results. An explanation for how this method works has not yet been found. Some parapsychologists have concluded that the area of the body that is ill undergoes a disturbance in "body electricity," and that the pendulum in some mysterious way detects this variation from the norm. Not all researchers agree with this theory, however, and most of them at present simply acknowledge that they do not understand how the pendulum works. Christians who have investigated this phenomenon are convinced that to some degree it belongs to the realm of the occultic, and that it should be avoided.

An exhaustive listing and discussion of all the physical phenomena that may be classified as magic are impossible in a work of this nature. But let us take time to look at one more example. The Chinese practice of acupuncture, which comes from ancient times, is receiving much publicity of late. Some of America's top medical men and biologists have watched Chinese doctors perform major surgery using this needle treatment as the anesthesia. In addition, doctors of dozens of countries have reported that with acupuncture they are successfully treating people with ulcers, colitis, rheumatism, arthritis, asthma, eczema, hypertension, diabetes, urinary tract infections, anxiety, and even some cases of blindness and deafness. The scientific world is at an utter loss to explain how acupuncture works. The Chinese say that our bodies contain two "life forces" known as Yin and Yang, and that the insertion and manipulation of the needles in any one of several hundred specific points interrupts the flow of one element or increases the flow of the other to correct any malfunction and restore well-being. Exponents of acupuncture generally agree that it is completely ineffective in healing fractures, curing cancer, overcoming infectious diseases, or repairing organs that have been severely damaged. These limitations suggest that even though acupuncture is "magical" in that it cannot be explained in terms of scientific knowledge, it should not be classified as occultic. Remember, we have no right to assert dogmatically that phenomena of this nature are necessarily the result of miraculous activity on the part of either God or the devil. Christians should be careful to avoid making assertions that cannot be substantiated.

Strange manifestations often take place in the realm of the psychical. We already have referred to visions, trance-speaking, automatic writing, materializations, and apparitions in our discussion of spiritism. This latter phenomenon can be distinguished from hallucinations because large groups of people have reported seeing apparitions or ghosts. Some even have been photographed. In substantiation of the above statement, let us note what Dr. Unger writes:

> Such forms have been represented by flash camera in Baron Schrenck-Notzing's Exhaustive Work *Materialisationphanomene, a Contribution to the Mediumistic Teleplastics* (Munich: Reinhardt, plates 23-30, p. 237)! The phenomena of materialization are also treated in the work of the French writer, Madame Bisson, *Les Phenomenes dits de Materialisation* (Paris 12th ed.) (Unger, *Demons in the World Today,* pp. 35, 54).

Raphael Gasson in *The Challenging Counterfeit* devotes several pages to this subject, and when one reads the body of literature that comes from the pen of both Christians and unbelievers, he realizes that all the reports of mysterious rappings and frightful specters cannot be lightly set aside as the product of overwrought imaginations or of tricksters. Christians who have studied in this field are convinced that at least in some of the cases the work of evil spirits can be detected, but again we must acknowledge that we do not at the present time know exactly how to account for all such phenomena.

The same admission must be made regarding extra-sensory perception in general. Research in this field by outstanding scholars like Professor J. B. Rhine, originally of Duke University, indicates that some people are able to perceive facts through a so-called "sixth sense," and that others have the ability to transfer their thoughts without using the usual methods of communication.

The mere possession of this "sixth sense," however, does not account for all the incidents involving ESP encountered by researchers. Parapsychologists are forced to acknowledge that an element of mystery exists bordering on the supernatural, for they have produced strong documentary evidence for astounding events that baffle the mind. Hundreds of people who were interviewed told of having vivid dreams in which they "saw" in the most minute detail and with absolute accuracy what was happening to a friend or loved one at the very moment the incident was taking place, sometimes thousands of miles away. Joost A. M. Meerlo in *Hidden Communion, Studies in the Communication Theory of Telepathy* sets forth a convincing case for the reality of such phenomena. The unbelieving scientist will insist that supernatural beings have nothing to do with any of the unexplained aspects of ESP. The Christian, on the other hand, realizing that a real world of invisible spiritual beings does exist, knows it is at least possible that they are involved. At this point, most believers who have investigated this subject are convinced that people who try to cultivate these faculties usually do so to their spiritual harm. Therefore every Christian must be extremely careful, and studiously avoid anything that may take him into areas forbidden by God.

Scientific research also has been unable to find an explanation for some well-documented speech occurences. The so-called charismatic movement in our own country with its emphasis upon speaking in tongues has focused a great deal of attention upon this subject. Many people in Christian churches believe they are reproducing the gift of tongues reported in the book of Acts and discussed by the apostle Paul in his first letter to the believers in Corinth. The Biblical soundness of their belief lies outside the scope of this study, but we can report that scientifically conducted investigations have shown all instances of tongues-speaking to have the same characteristics wherever they are encountered. Dr. George J. Jennings, in an extremely well-documented article published by the *Journal of the American Scientific Affiliation,* March, 1968, entitled "An Ethnological Study of Glossalalia," contends that the variation between the tongues spoken in a state of hysterical frenzy among primitives is only superficially different from that practiced in a quiet, composed Christian setting. He considers that all tongues experiences are a means by which uneasy and unsatisfied people identify with the supernatural, securing psychological compensation for the spiritual vacuum in which they live. Some Christian scholars believe that added to the psychological element is the possibility that demons are involved in tongues-speaking, but results of investigations in this field are not yet conclusive.

The kind of tongues-speaking to which Dr. Jennings refers in the article mentioned above is "language of ecstasy"; that is, articulated sounds which do not constitute an actual language. Reports keep coming of an even more astonishing phenomenon —speaking a real dialect that was never learned. Hundreds of missionaries, especially those working among oriental people, report that they often have encountered the mysterious ability of natives to speak in real languages that they never knew. These accounts come from Christian workers who represent widely divergent opinions regarding the charismatic movement. V. Raymond Edman, late Chancellor of Wheaton College, says,

> One of our Wheaton graduates who was born and reared on the Tibetan border tells of hearing the Tibetan monks in their ritual dances speak in English with quotations from Shakespeare, with profanity like drunken soldiers, or in German and French, or in languages unknown. Quite recently, a retired missionary told me of the same experience (*Christian Herald,* "Divine or Devilish," May, 1964, p. 16).

Reports of this nature are so numerous and come from such reputable people that one cannot set them aside lightly. Christians must not jump to hasty conclusions on such delicate and complicated subjects, but they certainly must recognize the possibility of demonic activity and exercise extreme caution in an attitude of prayerful dependence upon God. We will be able to analyze these reports far more adequately after they have been thoroughly researched by competent investigators.

In summary, research teams have found that many of the physical and psychical phenomena declared impossible by the rationalistic scientists of the early 1900's actually do take place. Most researchers do not even pretend to have a full explanation of how or why these occurrences transpire, but Christians are aware that some of them may be the result of evil spirits who work under the control of Satan. Regarding the occultic, the believer should walk the pathway of extreme caution. He should avoid any so-called magic that claims to bestow unusual knowledge or power through a psychic gift or ritualistic performances. It goes without saying that he must keep a safe distance from any form of black magic, and that he must examine carefully the doctrinal teaching of anyone who purports to provide healing or other temporal benefits in the name of the Lord.

Biblical faith is built upon trust in God and expresses itself in submission to His will. Every follower of Christ should be wary of magical cures and all outward demonstrations of allegedly supernatural power. As children of God, we must remember that we "walk by faith, not by sight" (2 Cor. 5:7), and that the faith that pleases God is "the assurance of things hoped for, a conviction of things not seen" (literal rendering of Heb. 11:1). We must not succumb to the temptation to find evidence for our faith through the senses. When we received Christ, we were brought into a vital union with Him, and the apostle Peter was writing to us when he said, "Whom, having not seen, ye love; in whom, though now ye see him not, yet believing, ye rejoice with joy unspeakable and full of glory" (1 Pet. 1:8).

Conclusion

This book has not been written merely to entertain its readers. Nor is its primary purpose the presentation of interesting facts and theories about occultism. Its intention is to instruct and warn believers so they will not become ensnared in the traps of Satan and his followers. Just as the devil enticed Eve with the prospect of gaining desirable knowledge and enviable pleasure by eating the forbidden fruit, so he also tempts God's children today to break through the limits the Lord has established. He makes the attractions of the world, even those which violate God's holy law, appear to be desirable and pleasurable. When the believer discovers the emptiness of this world's enchantments, Satan tries to deceive him into accepting false religious teaching or seeking spiritual help through some form of occultism. Through these devices the devil and his organization of evil spirits attempt to bring defeat and misery into the lives of God's children.

Satan is unable to harm a believer, however, if that person accepts the instruction of the Bible, maintains a life of prayer, submits himself to God, and resists the devil. An assured and obedient believer will avoid all occultic practices which promise information about the future or "miraculous" help for pressing problems. He also will carefully measure the teachings of all self-styled spokesmen for God by the truths of the Bible, and will feel no need for the benefits promised by cultists or occultic practitioners.

Though assured of salvation, the instructed believer will not become arrogant or self-confident. He knows full well that Satan and his followers constitute a formidable foe. Paul declared,

> For we wrestle not against flesh and blood, but against principalities, against powers, against the rulers of the darkness of this world, against spiritual wickedness in high places (Eph. 6:12).

No Christian should have a defeatist attitude, however, for God enables every believer to live a joyous life of victory over Satan and his forces. James said,

> Submit yourselves, therefore, to God. Resist the devil, and he will flee from you (James 4:7).

We are controlled by the Holy Spirit to the measure that we yield ourselves to God, and He empowers us to resist Satan effectively. In addition, God has outfitted us with a full panoply of armor by which we can both defend ourselves from the attacks of the forces of evil and take the offensive against them. The apostle Paul, using the figure of a warrior prepared for battle, lists these articles in Ephesians 6.

> Wherefore, take unto you the whole armor of God, that ye may be able to withstand in the evil day, and having done all, to stand.
> Stand, therefore, having your loins girded about with truth, and having on the breastplate of righteousness,
> And your feet shod with the preparation of the gospel of peace;
> Above all, taking the shield of faith, with which ye shall be able to quench all the fiery darts of the wicked.
> And take the helmet of salvation, and the sword of the Spirit, which is the word of God (Eph. 6:13-17).

Paul exhorts us to have our "loins girded about with truth." This belt refers to our sincerity, our honesty. No one will successfully resist and overcome the evil influence of Satan and his armies if he is hypocritical and dishonest. Remember, the devil is the father of lies. The child of God must not merely say that he desires victory over sin, but must truly long for it. He is to hate sin and manifest genuine earnestness. His spiritual vows and public statements must always be sincerely spoken, for the devil has no difficulty in defeating the hypocritical and half-hearted.

The breastplate of righteousness represents the believer's way of living. The Christian who desires to ward off the attacks of Satan and evil spirits must consciously choose a life of obedience, moral rectitude, and devout holiness. How is this life that pleases God to be attained? Largely by a humble determination to obey the exhortations of the Scriptures. The obedient believer's life is characterized by righteousness, and his testimony is effective to the winning of the lost and the crippling of Satan's power. The devil trembles at the sight of a truly godly person.

The Christian also is to have his "feet shod with the preparation of the gospel of peace." This means that he is to bear God's good news. He is to be a witness to others of the peace and joy that came to him when he placed his trust in Christ. The believer who does not bear a testimony loses spiritual keenness and becomes vulnerable to Satan's attacks.

The "shield of faith" speaks of strong belief nourished through daily prayer, Bible study, and spiritual activity. True faith accepts God's forgiveness with thankfulness, and exercises implicit trust in every time of trial and temptation. Without this

confidence in the Lord we would be spiritual weak-
lings, but with it we are the victors. John said,

> . . . and this is the victory that overcometh the
> world, even our faith (1 John 5:4).

The "helmet of salvation" describes the believer's
knowledge of his redemption. God's child should
rejoice in the assurance of a real, present, and personal salvation. He should remind himself daily
that he has been redeemed, that he has passed from
death to life, and that he is no longer under condemnation. The devil cannot effectively tempt a
Christian who is actively living a joyful Christian
life.

The child of God also must wield a weapon of
offense: the sword of the spirit, the Word of God.
Through the use of the Scriptures, he can resist
Satan's onslaughts successfully.

Child of God, you are on the winning side. You
have become "a partaker of the divine nature" (2
Pet. 1:4), through the new birth, and your body
has become the "temple of the Holy Spirit" (1 Cor.
6:19). Remember, "greater is he that is in you,
than he that is in the world" (1 John 4:4). God
has given you all you need for a happy and victorious Christian life now. He has explicitly declared that the power of the devil already has been
broken (Heb. 2:14, 15), and that someday you
will be delivered from the presence of sin and the
possibility of temptation. The apostle John, speaking of God's eternal city, assures us, "And there
shall in no way enter into it anything that defileth,
neither he that worketh abomination, or maketh a
lie" (Rev. 21:27). What a wonderful prospect!

Let me address a final word to the reader who
has not yet become a child of God. I hope the
reading of this book has shown you the reality of

Satan and his kingdom of evil. I pray that you will desire deliverance from sin, and that you will humbly acknowledge your need of Christ. Remember, one of two destinations awaits you — Heaven or Hell. To ignore Jesus Christ is to make impossible your entrance into Heaven. To receive Him as Savior is to guarantee a safe and successful journey into everlasting bliss. Jesus Himself declared,

> I am the door; by me if any man enter in, he shall be saved (John 10:9).

Why not bow your head in prayer right now and settle this matter of your salvation? Here is a suggested prayer you might offer: "Lord Jesus, I know I am a sinner and can never save myself. I realize that my own evil nature and the power of Satan and his forces are too much for me to handle in my own strength. I believe that You died for me and that You arose again from the dead. I am now receiving You as my Savior, my Lord, and my only hope of salvation. Amen." If you prayed this and really meant it, you are now a child of God. Your life will change, as you receive strength to do the will of God. The Bible assures you, "For whosoever shall call upon the name of the Lord shall be saved" (Rom. 10:13).

Richard W. De Haan

Epilogue

The reader may wish to engage in further and more detailed study on the subject discussed in this book. Therefore, the following annotated listing of some relatively non-technical books is offered for your help.

Dr. Merrill F. Unger is the author of *Biblical Demonology* (Van Kampen Press, 1952), an excellent study of the Biblical material dealing with Satan and evil spirits. He also has written *Demons in the World Today* (Tyndale House Publishers, 1971), in which he relates occultic practices of our present day to the Scriptures. A third work by the same author on this general subject is entitled *The Haunting of Bishop Pike* (Tyndale House Publishers, 1971). Dr. Unger is a highly respected Old Testament scholar, and his books contain excellent bibliographies for the student who is equipped to do extensive research.

Dr. Kurt Koch, a German theologian with considerable technical knowledge in the fields of medicine, psychiatry, and parapsychology, is perhaps the best source of case histories and other factual data relating to the practice of occultism. He has devoted over thirty years of his life to this study, and has personally investigated more than 20,000 incidents in which psychic and occultic phenomena were involved. A number of valuable books have come from his pen, and the most helpful are: *Christian Counseling and Occultism; Between Christ and Satan;* and *Occult Bondage and Deliverance.* They are published by Kregel of Grand Rapids.

Joseph Bayly has produced a readable and valuable paperback entitled, *What About Horoscopes?* (David C. Cook Publishing Company, 1970). It includes a helpful glossary in which he gives a brief but accurate definition of the words and terms generally used in occultic literature.

Raphael Gasson, a medium who came to know the Lord Jesus Christ, has written what Dr. Unger calls "a brilliant and firsthand expose of spiritualism" entitled *The Challenging Counterfeit* (Logos International, 1966).

Victor H. Ernest, a highly respected pastor in a conservative denomination, has recently published a work entitled *I Talked With Spirits* (Tyndale House Publishers, 1970). Rev. Ernest grew up in a home where spiritualism was practiced and became deeply involved in it himself, but was later led to faith in Christ.

John L. Nevius, a Presbyterian missionary in China at the close of the nineteenth century, recorded his experiences and observations in a large work entitled *Demon Possession and Allied Themes.* This book has been considered a classic in the field, and has been reprinted recently under the title *Demon Possession* (Kregel Publications, 1968.)

Mrs. Penn-Lewis and Evan Roberts produced a work entitled *War on the Saints* (London: Marshall Brothers, 1912).

In addition to the above books, all of which are the products of believers, one might wish to study some of the works which do not approach this field from the presuppositions of the Christian faith.

Joost A. M. Meerlo, Associate Professor of Psychiatry at New York School of Psychiatry, is the author of a work entitled *Hidden Communion,*

Studies in the Communication Theory of Telepathy (Garrett Publications, 1964).

J. B. Rhine began a series of experiments in the area of mental telepathy at Duke University in 1927, and today a report of what he and a number of other collaborators discovered can be found in *Extra-Sensory Perception After Sixty Years* (Crescendo Publishers, 1967).

Bishop James A. Pike, with Diane Kennedy, tells the story of the experiences which led him to attend seances through which he purportedly established contact with his dead son in a book, *The Other Side* (Dell Publishing Company, 1969).

Extensive bibliographies are available in a number of scholarly works. Any person who wishes to do exhaustive research in this field will find no shortage of material. One should be careful, however, not to become too engrossed in this subject, especially if he is inclined to suffer from mental or spiritual depression.

Herbert Vander Lugt